T0147020

WHOLE

A Guided Workbook of Life

SHALAN LANDRY

WESTBOW
PRESS®
A DIVISION OF THOMAS NELSON
& ZONDERVAN

WestBow Press books may be ordered through booksellers or by contacting:

WestBow Press
A Division of Thomas Nelson & Zondervan
1663 Liberty Drive
Bloomington, IN 47403
www.westbowpress.com
844-714-3454

ISBN: 978-1-6642-6704-6 (sc)
ISBN: 978-1-6642-6703-9 (e)

Library of Congress Control Number: 2022909202

Print information available on the last page.

WestBow Press rev. date: 08/23/2022

CONTENTS

INTRODUCTION

Whole. What comes to mind when you think of this word? Let's look at some definitions of the word "whole."

Whole

- *all of; entire*
- *in an unbroken or undamaged state; in one piece*
- *a thing that is complete in itself*
- *all of something*

When we think of the word "whole," we often think of items or stuff, like a whole slice of a three-layered double-chocolate cake, a whole pepperoni pizza with extra cheese, or a whole pint of ice cream. There are even positive sayings about items that are not whole or full. *Look at the glass half full, not half empty. Something is better than nothing at all.* We think of stuff when we think of whole, but what comes to mind when you examine yourself with regard to the definition of "whole"? What about the positive sayings about having a piece of something or incompleteness? Will having healthy pieces of yourself ever equal an abundant life?

Let's go back to the definition of "whole" and consider what it looks like in an individual. An individual who is whole is unbroken, is undamaged, not lacking, and is in one piece. He or she is full and complete without the help or need of any other person or item. So after a formal definition and in the context described, do you consider yourself whole?

Well, I'll be honest. There was a time when I was not whole. In fact, I was broken to the point where I was unrecognizable to the people closest to me. I didn't even recognize myself. The harsh reality of this world can really get to us if we allow it. That's what happened to me. I was an intelligent, all-star student, a well-traveled, cultured, and college-educated child of God, but I was on the road to destruction. It could happen to anyone. However, everyone, no matter how broken, has the opportunity to be made whole and live a life of gratitude and purpose! That's good news!

You may be familiar with the Hebrew term *shalom*. Even though we see it used as "hello" and "goodbye," it actually translates to wholeness, peace, tranquility, completeness, harmony, and prosperity (*Online Etymology Dictionary*, 2021). Close your eyes and imagine a *whole* you. Imagine your heart being so filled with love, peace, and harmony that it overflows to the people around you. Imagine waking up every morning and laying your head down every night with a smile on your face and a heart filled with gratitude and peace.

This workbook will lay out the principles you need to

1. discover and redefine who you are;
2. address and release your insecurities, current pain, and the pain of your past;
3. transform or renew your mindset; and
4. excel into your purpose.

Remember that this is a process, and it will not happen overnight. It may be difficult as we live in a time that is filled with instant gratification—fast food, same-day shipping, digital photos, downloadable applications, and information literally in the palm of our hands have spoiled us to wanting what we want *now*. It will take time, work, and consistency. This workbook is a guide that requires you to find yourself in the knowledge on these pages through various activities. So be honest because you will discover that your words will be an important reference in your process. Your comments, notes, and answers will bring this book to life for you as it can be used as a plan of action for your life. Also, please use the resources in the back of this workbook as you progress. Each resource is categorized by topic in the text.

Let me be the first to commend you on your decision! Our will is the most powerful gift God has given us, and you have chosen to take the first step to become *whole*!

A PRAYER FOR THE READERS

Dear Heavenly Father,

First and foremost, thank you for being God, Lord and Savior, my Deliverer, and so much more. I pray that the words in this workbook serve as a catalyst for your people to escort them toward the road to healing, wholeness, and joy so that they may better serve you by living out the purpose you have for them. I pray that every word resonates with each individual and that they find themselves in this workbook. Help them to move into their purpose one step at a time, day by day.

I speak life onto each individual. Thank you in advance for the transformation, the deliverance, healing, and joy that will emerge. Thank you for the liberation from spiritual bondage and the broken chains that will ensue. Lord, someone has felt like they were imprisoned or trapped but will be set free in the name of Jesus!

I thank you and I praise your Holy Name.

It is in Jesus's name I pray.

Amen.

ACKNOWLEDGE WHO GOD IS

This is the basis of this entire journal because nothing can be done without acknowledging who He is. Better yet, nothing *should* be done without knowing and acknowledging who God is. We can maneuver and do things without acknowledging Him, but we set ourselves up for failure. Let's look at the word "acknowledge."

> Acknowledge—*to accept or admit the existence or truth of; to recognize the fact, importance, or quality of something or someone.*

Ask yourself these questions:

- Do I know who God is?
- Have I accepted God?
- Do I acknowledge God in everything I do?

We will spend some time exploring who God is, how to accept God as our Lord and Savior, and how to acknowledge Him in all we do.

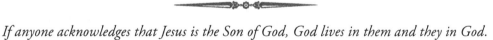

If anyone acknowledges that Jesus is the Son of God, God lives in them and they in God.
—1 John 4:15 (NIV)

I made this mistake for years. I knew God, had accepted Him as Lord and Savior, but I did not acknowledge Him. I was saved but not set free. I went through so many obstacles, land mines, traps, and dead-ends in the seasons of my life. Depression, anxiety attacks, digestive issues, and other illnesses plagued me—all because I didn't acknowledge Him. If I would have just acknowledged Him, He would have made my path straight.

In all thy ways acknowledge him, and he shall direct thy paths.
—Proverbs 3:6 (KJV)

Again, I was saved and knew who God was at the time. I didn't understand that when we acknowledge God, it reminds us of who He is, and it leads us to recognize that our situation is insignificant compared to Him. No situation is ever a match for God. Once I began to acknowledge God, those obstacles seemed easier to overcome, and my path became more defined. Some of the troubles that I had were still there, but they weren't as difficult to endure, and I had peace. My health improved, and I became more productive. Notice that I still had trouble. That is one thing that God declared.

I have told you these things, so that in me you may have peace. In this world
you will have trouble. But take heart! I have overcome the world.
—John 16:33 (NIV)

This brings me back to the importance of knowing Him. Looking back on the definition of "acknowledge," is it possible to acknowledge Him without first knowing who He is? I'll help you. That would be a *no*.

Every topic, activity, and reflection in this workbook goes back to knowing and acknowledging who God is. So let's get started with studying the Bible, the Word of God. We will explore who God is so that we can acknowledge Him in everything we do. I'm living proof that it makes a difference.

GOD IS LOVE (PART 1)

ove. What is your definition of love? Is it a warm and fuzzy feeling? Is it a feeling at all? The dictionary lists three definitions of the word "love."

- It is an intense feeling of deep affection. For example, babies fill their parents with feelings of love.
- It is a great interest and pleasure in something. An example of this would be how my aunt Cynthia loves watching the Dallas Cowboys play football.
- It is the feeling of deep romantic attachment to someone, as in being in love with a significant other.

What do these three definitions have in common? Well, each has a level of self-absorption, as it is all about how the individual *feels*, which makes it conditional and unstable. This is how families can become estranged. It is why there are bandwagon sports fans and why people lose interest in hobbies. It is also why people "fall in and out of love" with each other. These examples of the word "love" are based on feelings, expectations, and emotions.

So if the dictionary definition of love displays that it is conditional, unstable, self-absorbed, and emotional, why would the Bible declare (multiple times) that "God is love"? This would mean that God is unstable, selfish, emotional, and deals in conditions, which is a complete falsehood.

A complete falsehood is a whopping understatement!

Instead, the world's view of love is gravely skewed. The Word of God not only declares that God is Love, but it also tells what Love is and what Love is not.

⁴ Love is patient, love is kind. It does not envy, it does not boast, it is not proud. ⁵ It does not dishonor others, it is not self-seeking, it is not easily angered, it keeps no record of wrongs. ⁶ Love does not delight in evil but rejoices with the truth. ⁷ It always protects, always trusts, always hopes, always perseveres. ⁸ Love never fails. But where there are prophecies, they will cease; where there are tongues, they will be stilled; where there is knowledge, it will pass away.
—1 Corinthians 13:4–8 (NIV)

There is no fear in love. But perfect love drives out fear, because fear has to do with punishment. The one who fears is not made perfect in love.
—1 John 4:18 (NIV)

Activity #1a

"God is Love." What else do the scriptures say Love *is* or *does*? Complete the list below.

1. _____   6. _____
2. _____   7. _____
3. _____   8. _____
4. _____   9. _____
5. _____   10. _____

Activity #1b

What does the Bible say Love is *not* or does *not* do? Complete the list below.

1. _____   6. _____
2. _____   7. _____
3. _____   8. _____
4. _____   9. _____
5. _____   10. _____

Review your lists. Do you see the difference in the world's view of love and how the Word of God defines Love? The Word of God tells us that we are from God and not of the world. So we are to adhere to *His* Word.

Love is a command, which means that it is an action, not a feeling. In 1 John 4:21, God commands us to love one another.

And he has given us this command: Anyone who loves God must also love their brother and sister.

—1 John 4:21 (NIV)

I will illustrate this further. A feeling is an emotion. For example, I can be happy, sad, excited, etc. Can we shift our emotions at will? There is such a thing as emotional intelligence, which is not what I am referring to. Emotional intelligence is the ability to be aware of and express emotions in a sensible way. If you are devastated by a life-changing event, can you switch from devastated and distraught to ecstatic and excited when prompted to do so? Let's try it. One … two … three … I command you to get happy! Go!

It doesn't work, does it? It's not supposed to because emotions are inexorable, thereby, a part of life. The bottom line of this example is that Love is an action, not a feeling or emotion.

GOD IS LOVE (PART 2)

We discussed that Love is an action in God is Love (part 1). So God is action.

I have a quick question for you. Would you willingly give your child (or a loved one you hold dear) up to die to possibly save people that you know will repeatedly disrespect and offend you?

I'm going to be completely honest with you. If someone asked me this question, my answer would be a resounding "No" before he or she even finished the question! I imagine it would be along the lines of

"Would you willingly give your child up..."

"NO!" (Harshly)

How about you? I'm willing to wager that I'm not alone. *But* this is exactly what God did! He *sacrificed* His *only* son to die to give us the opportunity or choice to be saved from eternal damnation knowing that we will sin against Him!

For God so loved the world that he gave his one and only Son, that
whoever believes in him shall not perish but have eternal life.
—John 3:16 (NIV)

[3] *He was despised and rejected by mankind, a man of suffering, and familiar with pain. Like one from whom people hide their faces he was despised, and we held him in low esteem.* [4] *Surely he took up our pain and bore our suffering, yet we considered him punished by God, stricken by him, and afflicted.* [5] *But he was pierced for our transgressions, he was crushed for our iniquities; the punishment that brought us peace was on him, and by his wounds we are healed.*
—Isaiah 53:3–5 (NIV)

The price for sinning or immorality is death. So God incarnated Himself on earth (Jesus). Jesus, who had *never* sinned, became sin ... *all* our past, present, and future sins. Then, He was tortured beyond measure. Brokenhearted, He died on the cross and was resurrected so that when we die, our spirit can have the opportunity to resurrect and live eternally in heaven, the kingdom of God. He continuously reveals His Love for us through His actions.

———◆◦◆———

For the wages of sin is death; but the gift of God is eternal life through Jesus Christ our Lord.
—Romans 6:23 (KJV)

———◆◦◆———

Activity #2

Sacrifice is a selfless act. Review your lists from Activity #1. Remember, God is Love, and He dwells within us. Seek out ways to reflect qualities of Love in your daily life. Write down at least five acts of Love you can strive to do on a regular basis.

1. _____

2. _____

3. _____

4. _____

5. _____

A sacrifice is an act of giving up something of value for something that is prioritized as more worthy or of more importance. Again, it is selflessness, or "less of self," which may require acts like giving up one's time, energy, or resources.

The main takeaway is that God is Love, and Love is not a feeling, but an action.

GOD IS KING OF KINGS

It's important to know and remember that the Bible is about the King (God), His kingdom, God's goal of extending His kingdom, and God's embodiment of Himself (Jesus) sent to restore kings to His kingdom (Dr. Myles Munroe). The goal of God is to reestablish His kingdom on earth. Let's review the following scriptures:

The kingdom of heaven is like a king who prepared a wedding banquet for his son.
—Matthew 22:2 (NIV)

Then the King will say to those on his right, 'Come, you who are blessed by my Father; take your inheritance, the kingdom prepared for you since the creation of the world.
—Matthew 25:34 (NIV)

Therefore, the kingdom of heaven is like a king who wanted to settle accounts with his servants.
—Matthew 18:23 (NIV)

Notice that Jesus's references to God were about a king and His kingdom. God chose to identify Himself as a king. So in order to understand God and His Word, we must explore the terms "king" and "kingdom." It is important for us to explore this because we were created in His image. The more we know about God, the more we know about ourselves. This leads me to this question: If God is the King and we were made in His image and likeness, then what are we? God is the king of kings. Hence, we are royalty! Let's look at the dictionary's definition of "king."

King—the male ruler of an independent state who inherits his position by right of birth

This is important to remember because this means that a king is not elected or voted in like a president, mayor, prime minister, etc. A king is a king because he is born into the position. So God is identifying Himself with a king state that no one contributed to. Neither did anyone give Him His position. He is a ruler in His own right. Now let's discuss the qualities and nature of a king.

All kings have glory. The glory of a king is what expresses his nature. The word "glory" is the term *kabod* or *kavod* (Hebrew) in the Old Testament of the Bible and *doxa* (Greek) in the New Testament, which means the full weight of, essence, or nature of something (*Online Etymology Dictionary*, 2021).

A characteristic of kings is that they love to show what they are like through their actions. Therefore, God has a nature and shows it through His actions and works. An example of this would be how God's actions gained glory through Pharaoh and his army in Exodus 14. God led the Israelites out of the hands of Pharaoh, the king of Egypt, through Moses. Pharaoh and his army's hearts were hardened and did not listen to Moses when he told him to let the Israelites go. God acted so they could know what He is like, His glory. God said this:

¹⁷ I will harden the hearts of the Egyptians so that they will go in after them. And I will gain glory through Pharaoh and all his army, through his chariots and his horsemen. ¹⁸ The Egyptians will know that I am the Lord when I gain glory through Pharaoh, his chariots and his horsemen."
—Exodus 14:17–18 (NIV)

Furthermore, God leaves evidence behind for us to know His nature. When I am stressed, I love taking walks on an open trail to take in all the things that God has created. I breathe in the air that God has made and has kept at the perfect molecular formula for our existence. As I feel the breeze blowing and the warmth of the sun on my face, I am reminded of how God keeps the planets in systematic orbit around the sun and keeps planet Earth rotating and orbiting at a safe distance away from the sun for us to live. Then I look around at the trees dancing and singing in the breeze as if they were glorifying Him as well. Even the birds, crickets, and grasshoppers sing His praises. I marvel at the open sky and clouds and cannot help but give God glory. And an immense calmness overcomes me because I realize that my God is bigger than any issue or situation I could ever face. Finally, I see people, and all are unique. It makes me realize that there are about 8 billion people on this earth and no two are exactly alike, which lets me know that we are also the glory of God. We are an important aspect of God's glory because we are His works, His creation. Again, He made us in His image. So we are kings and queens.

One of the most famous kings in the Bible, King David, wrote Psalm 8. David was a great king, but even he knew that God is the King of Kings and Ruler of All!

¹ Lord, our Lord, how majestic is your name in all the earth! You have set your glory in the heavens.
² Through the praise of children and infants you have established a stronghold
against your enemies, to silence the foe and the avenger.
³ When I consider your heavens, the work of your fingers, the
moon and the stars, which you have set in place,
⁴ what is mankind that you are mindful of them, human beings that you care for them? ⁵ You
have made them a little lower than the angels and crowned them with glory and honor.
⁶ You made them rulers over the works of your hands;
you put everything under their feet:
⁷ all flocks and herds, and the animals of the wild,
⁸ the birds in the sky, and the fish in the sea, all that swim the paths of the seas.
⁹ Lord, our Lord, how majestic is your name in all the earth!
—Psalm 8 (NIV)

Have you ever noticed that kings live in extravagant castles? Why do you think that is? Kings build and decorate castles to display their splendor. The luxuriousness of a castle serves the purpose of revealing the personality and glory of the king, even when the king is not visible. People can admire a castle from far away and be in awe of it when they approach it. Guess what, the Bible declares that God dwells in us! So when people approach us, they are automatically supposed to know who we belong to. God wants to bless us so well that people hasten to Him. The dilemma with some people is that they don't believe that God dwells in them. This is because they don't know God, which is why it is so important to study His Word and have a close relationship with God so that we can discern His voice when He speaks.

And what agreement hath the temple of God with idols? for ye are the
temple of the living God; as God hath said, I will dwell in them, and walk
in them; and I will be their God, and they shall be my people:
—2 Corinthians 6:16 (KJV)

Activity #3

We are to glorify God in all we do. What are some things you can do to glorify God? List three things below. If you are uncertain, you *can* come back to this activity later to complete it.

1. _____
   _____
2. _____
   _____
3. _____
   _____

The last quality we will discuss is a king's word. Why do you think God did not identify Himself as a president or a prime minister? Well, here's a follow-up question to help you answer that. Why does a president, prime minister, or other members of a government or parliament have checks and balances? It could take years for a president, mayor, or any other official to create a law. It must go through stages. However, the word of a king is law, and it constitutes his will. When a king declares something, it is made so without debate. No permission is required, and it is not up for discussion. So God's Word is always law, and He does not change His mind, nor does He eventually allow His Word to develop into something else. An example of this is the human body. We are descendants of Adam, whom God created. This illustration is laughable and outrageous, but please bear with me. What if 95 percent of the people in this world voted for our armpits to be relocated to behind our knees? Ninety-five percent of the world are in favor of it. However, God created us with armpits under the arm. Do you think people will be born with "kneepits" from henceforth because of the majority vote? Will the rest of our armpits migrate to the back of our knees over time? I think not!

² Obey the king's command, I say, because you took an oath before God. ³ Do not be in a hurry to leave the king's presence. Do not stand up for a bad cause, for he will do whatever he pleases. ⁴ Since a king's word is supreme, who can say to him, "What are you doing?"
—Ecclesiastes 8:2–4 (NIV)

Your word, LORD, is eternal; it stands firm in the heavens.
—Psalm 119:89 (NIV)

Reflection #1

First: Take a few minutes to look up the YouTube video link of Dr. Myles Munroe's, "The Kingdom of God Defined," to gain a clearer perspective of this section. The link is listed in the resources at the back of this workbook. Then: Write down your reflections and notes on what we have discussed thus far about God. What resonated with you? What are your takeaways?

_____

_____

_____

_____

_____

_____

_____

_____

_____

_____

_____

_____

_____

_____

_____

_____

_____

_____

_____

_____

_____

_____

_____

_____

_____

_____

_____

_____

_____

GOD IS OMNIPRESENT, OMNIPOTENT, AND OMNISCIENT

I take comfort in the above statement and subtitle. If He is everywhere, has seen and knows everything, and can do anything, there is absolutely nothing I can do to surprise Him. We cannot stump God.

---

¹ You have searched me, Lord, and you know me.
² You know when I sit and when I rise; you perceive my thoughts from afar.
³ You discern my going out and my lying down; you are familiar with all my ways.
⁴ Before a word is on my tongue you, Lord, know it completely.
⁵ You hem me in behind and before, and you lay your hand upon me.
⁶ Such knowledge is too wonderful for me, too lofty for me to attain.
⁷ Where can I go from your Spirit? Where can I flee from your presence?
⁸ If I go up to the heavens, you are there; if I make my bed in the depths, you are there.
⁹ If I rise on the wings of the dawn, if I settle on the far side of the sea,
¹⁰ even there your hand will guide me, your right hand will hold me fast.
¹¹ If I say, "Surely the darkness will hide me and the light become night around me,"
¹² even the darkness will not be dark to you; the night will shine
like the day, for darkness is as light to you.
—Psalm 139:1–12 (NIV)

God is *I am,* which sums up His omnipresence, omnipotence, and omniscience. God does not need anyone or anything to exist, and no one created Him. He does not have or require a source for His power and knowledge. He has no need for transportation devices, or even teleportation, to get from A to B because He is already there. He always was, always is, and always will be. God exists out of time and the universe, which is why our science and technology cannot explain Him or His works. He just … Is … and will be forevermore!

¹³ Moses said to God, "Suppose I go to the Israelites and say to them, 'The God of your fathers has sent me to you,' and they ask me, 'What is his name?' Then what shall I tell them?" ¹⁴ God said to Moses, "I AM WHO I AM. This is what you are to say to the Israelites: 'I AM has sent me to you.'"
—Exodus 3:13–14 (NIV)

I remember nearly losing my mind a few years ago trying to be everywhere at once. I was trying to hold a failing marriage together, take care of my daughter, keep the house up, and handle issues at work simultaneously. My husband was working in another state, my daughter was struggling in school and undergoing multiple disability tests, and there seemed to be constant conflict at my job. I remember praying to God to give me the strength and energy to do all the things that I needed to do. The key word is *needed* to do. That is where I went wrong. I took on and concerned myself with things that I did not have to take on or that were out of my control. I would fly to Colorado and drive to Wyoming in the dead of winter each week on my days off to try to rekindle my relationship with my husband. I would wash his clothes, clean his living space, and cook for the week. Then I would drive to the airport, fly home (Texas), and return to work with a wave of problems waiting for me. As soon as I clocked in, I was presented with a long list of situations to resolve that occurred on my days off. I literally walked around with this list, crossing things out as I resolved them. In addition to my actual job description, that list would take up 100 percent of my time. I would skip lunches and breaks and even work off the clock sometimes to complete work. My daughter, my sweet baby girl, was affected by all of this. My family would help with her as I worked twelve-hour shifts. They would help bring her to school and pick her up. She would spend the night at my mom's house, and I would come over after my shift to help her with homework, spend time with her, and put her to bed by 9:00 p.m. Then, I would go home to get ready for the next day, get about three hours of sleep, and do it all over again. We found out that my daughter has autism and suffers from depression and anxiety. I created lesson plans to help her with school, drafted accommodations guide packets for each of her teachers, and worked closely with her counselor and tutors to maximize her education. I handled repairs and maintenance at my house and voluntarily refinished the extra living space above the garage into a man cave for my husband for when he returned home. I went on like this every day for months. My health began to fail. I remember so vividly how it all came crashing down on me in a conversation in the car with my daughter on the way to school. We were discussing school and the lessons we were going to do in the summer. Suddenly, she started crying, and it startled me. Before I could say anything, my daughter told me that she was so sorry for letting me down and not being a good daughter, but she tried her best and she still failed a subject. That nearly ripped my heart out. I quickly replied, "No, sweetheart, I've failed you. I let you down. This is all my doing. So don't blame yourself. You are the best daughter anyone could ever ask or hope for."

After I dropped her off at school, I pulled over and wept. Then, I heard the Holy Spirit speaking to me, reminding me that there are some things I was not meant to carry. I am not God and cannot be everywhere at once. I must give it to God and trust that He is omnipresent, omnipotent, and omniscient and is able to handle anything I give Him. I am thankful that even though I am not able to be everywhere and handle everything all at once, I serve a mighty God that is!

Let's take a closer look at these three distinctive characteristics of God. First, it is important to note that the prefix *omni* is the Latin word for "all."

Omnipresent—All-present

Have you ever had to wait for someone to show up to do something for you? The availability of that individual is limited because he or she can only be in one place at a time. Take the situation I had where I was trying to do it all. While I was in Wyoming with my husband, my daughter was in Texas. So if an emergency arose, it would take hours for me to get to her. She would have to depend on someone else in her time of need. Well, God is omnipresent, meaning He is everywhere all the time. So you will never have to wait for Him to show up or arrive because He is already there.

Therefore, God does not move. He manifests or reveals Himself. He is far too great to be limited to movement. Movement suggests that He would leave one place to go to another. This would mean that He would have to leave you to come and see about me and vice versa, which limits His availability. Wherever we are and whatever the situation, God is already there!

The Lord himself goes before you and will be with you; he will never leave
you nor forsake you. Do not be afraid; do not be discouraged."
—Deuteronomy 31:8 (NIV)

Have I not commanded you? Be strong and courageous. Do not be afraid; do not
be discouraged, for the Lord your God will be with you wherever you go."
—Joshua 1:9 (NIV)

Activity #4a

I am grateful that I serve a God who is omnipresent because He has been and will continue to be there for me, especially in my darkest, lowest hour. List why you are grateful that God is omnipresent below. If you are uncertain, you *can* come back to this activity later to complete it.

_____
_____
_____
_____

Omniscient—All-knowing

I have always had a D-type epistemic curiosity. I obtain knowledge out of fear of knowledge deprivation. It takes me a while to decide on things because I research every aspect of the situation or question prior to deciding. I even go as far as poking holes into my research and formulating questions for those limitations to answer and resolve so that I won't have to deal with any surprises. It sounds time-consuming, right? Well, it is. Oftentimes, time would expire before I could make a decision. When I did make a timely decision, I would continue to research and stress over the unknown and the potential consequences of my decision. I used to find myself stressing over things that may happen and how things may end up. I missed out on blessings, opportunities, and abundance by obsessing over the unknown. The truth is, none of us knows or will ever know everything, but I serve a God who does!

As I stated, God is everywhere all the time. This includes knowing our past, present, and future. I had to come to that realization. God is my Father. He Loves me and wants the best for me. So if God knows what happened in my past, what's currently going on with me, and what will happen in my future, and He is all-powerful, why am I stressing?

Activity #4b

I take comfort in knowing that God is my Heavenly Father, He Loves me, knows every detail in my past, present, and future, and cannot be bewildered about what goes on in this world. List why God's omniscience is or would be beneficial to you in your life below. If you are uncertain, you *can* come back to this activity later to complete it.

_____
_____
_____
_____

Omnipotent—All-potent (powerful)

In studying the word "potent," I discovered something rather interesting. The alteration of the word "potent," "potence," means "crutch" in Medieval Latin, Late Middle English, and Old French. As you know, a crutch is used to support the lame or an individual that is unable to walk normally because of an injury or illness of the leg or foot. God is *omni*potent. In keeping with the translation "crutch," He is more than just a crutch. A crutch carries some of your weight. Remember, "omni" means "all." Not only is God able to support you, but He can also carry you ... *all* of you! The Bible does not say, "Cast *some* of your care on Him," but cast them *all* on Him. He is more than capable of handling every care from us *all*.

*⁶ Therefore humble yourselves under the mighty hand of God, that He may exalt you in due time, ⁷ casting **all** your care upon Him, for He cares for you.*
—1 Peter 5:6–7 (NKJV)

*²⁸ "Come to me, **all** you who are weary and burdened, and I will give you rest. ²⁹ Take my yoke upon you and learn from me, for I am gentle and humble in heart, and you will find rest for your souls. ³⁰ For my yoke is easy and my burden is light."*
—Matthew 11:28–30 (NIV)

*¹⁰ So do not fear, for I am with you; do not be dismayed, for I am your God. I will strengthen you and help you; I will uphold you with my righteous right hand. ¹¹ "All who rage against you will surely be ashamed and disgraced; those who oppose you will be as nothing and perish. ¹² Though you search for your enemies, you will not find them. Those who wage war against you will be as nothing at all. ¹³ For I am the L*ORD *your God who takes hold of your right hand and says to you, Do not fear; I will help you.*
—Isaiah 41:10–13 (NIV)

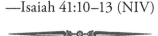

That got me fired up because it got me thinking about myself! I am so thankful that God was there when my spiritual and mental injuries and illnesses caused my spiritual feet to stumble in life and my legs to grow weary. He was there to pick me up off the ground and support me when I fell flat on my face. He has been my support, more than a crutch, and His power is made perfect in my weakness.

Activity #5

Let's lean on God. Have you been trying to do it all on your own? We all need God. He will never give us a life that makes Him unnecessary. List and give a brief description of things you need to begin trusting God with. If you are uncertain, you *can* come back to this activity later to complete.

1. _____
   _____

2. _____
   _____

3. _____
   _____

4. _____
   _____

5. _____
   _____

The Word of God tells us not to lean on our own understanding but to completely rely on or trust in Him wholeheartedly (Prov. 3:5, NKJV). We discussed that God is omnipresent; He is with us everywhere we go. We rely on Him; He is our support as an individual who clings to a crutch. Remember, God said that we will have trouble in our lives, but He has already overcome them all. So God is the answer to every issue, circumstance, or trouble we could ever have. Addictions or bad habits may be directly correlated to a lack of connection and longing for God, whether we know it or not. The longer the disconnect with God, the deeper the emptiness and longing for God, and the worse the addictions or unhealthy habits get.

Here is a practical example. My dad was an athlete and endured multiple sports injuries when he was younger. He was able to just shake them off and keep playing for a good while. As he got older, it got harder to shake those injuries off, and they began to noticeably show up in his daily life to people around him. He was stiff and moved slower than before; it impaired his game. At fifty, he underwent knee surgery. He was instructed to use a crutch for at least six weeks, but Dad doggedly said that he could walk on his own. By day 2, he was hopping, limping, and hobbling around on that leg. That knee never healed well. Four months later, he had surgery number 2 and still refused to utilize the crutch that was right there by his side. Surgery number 3 came only two months later. He bypassed the crutch. This time he hobbled and fell, causing further injury. At age fifty-two, the damage had gotten worse. His hobbling resulted in a full knee replacement. He went fishing on day 4 after that surgery (you guessed it, without the crutch). By this time, the lack of a crutch had resulted in a knee replacement for the other knee. In addition, he had multiple slipped disks and required hip replacements. Now, he is sixty-four years old, can barely walk or sit, and is in constant pain.

I bring this up because many of us are like my dad but in the spiritual realm. We think we can do it all on our own, and we bypass God, our crutch, our solid footing. What's worse is that some of us don't even realize that we are lame and hobbling, limping, and hopping through life as it has become our new normal. We don't have to do it by ourselves. In fact, we were never meant to do it by ourselves. The Bible says that He will never leave us or forsake us. Meaning, He will never give up on us or give us up. He is just waiting for us to cling to Him.

Let's Sum It Up!

We have discussed that God is Love and how He sacrificed His Son so that we can have eternal life. He is King *over all* kings and His authority, power, and knowledge are matchless and infinite. God is everywhere all the time; He is omnipresent. We cannot stump or shock Him because He is omniscient and all-knowing. And He is more than a crutch—He is all-powerful, omnipotent.

If you realize that you have been hobbling through life, trying to do it all by yourself, feel trapped, feel a void in your life, feel drained as if you have nothing left, know that you are not alone. Believe me, I have been there. I can't stress it enough. Hardships will arise, but I guarantee you that the battles you encounter will seem much smaller when you submit them to God and allow Him to fight for you.

THE INVITATION

As I mentioned earlier, God's goal is to recolonize the earth with the kingdom of God through mankind (Munroe, *The Kingdom of God Defined*, 2017). We are descendants of Adam. God gave humans dominion over the earth to mimic the culture of heaven. He formed Adam from the earth, which is why our bodies contain its elements (i.e., iron, magnesium, potassium, etc.). The name "Adam" derives from the Hebrew word *Adamah*, which means "the ground" or "earth." Then God built Eve from Adam's rib. They were both made in God's likeness and were blameless, or without sin. God gave Adam a law: "Do not eat anything from the Tree of Knowledge or you will die." Remember, the price of sin is death. The word "sin" in Hebrew is *asham*, which means "guilty of rebellion," or *hata*, meaning "to go astray." So sin is anything that rebels against God. When Adam rebelled against God or sinned by eating fruit from that tree, all of us who were inside him entered into sin with him. We inherited the spirit of rebellion. For example, do we have to teach a toddler to throw tantrums, fight, be selfish, or lie? It is already inside us because of Adam's first sin. God created death, but it could not kill yet. It only existed until it was activated by the sin of Adam. God always keeps His promises. He set the penalty for sin (death), but He created a way for us to be saved from that penalty.

Life and death of the body are in the blood. Think about it. Can we survive without blood? When we get a cut on our body, our blood works to heal it and create scar tissue to close the wound. Blood illnesses are usually terminal. Nutrients are carried in the blood. The blood protects the body (immune system). White blood cells fight off illnesses. All your organs are working for your blood.

We were all born from the same sinful, death-ridden bloodline. So mankind has a spiritual blood deficiency (Munroe, Understanding the Blood Covenant, 2019). Therefore, animal blood was used for atonement or sacrifice. Man's bloodline is contaminated; animals were used to cover man's sin temporarily as they were sacrificed at the altar. God created animals in case man sinned. None of us can save ourselves because we all are related in that way. It would be transferring contaminated blood into a body with equally contaminated blood. So we need someone who was not born of Man that does not have contaminated blood to give us a "blood transfusion" so that our bloodline can be restored. This is why God created a woman's womb in such a fashion. In normal circumstances, a woman can carry a baby and the baby's blood never touches or mixes with the mother's blood, which is how Mary carried the Son of God in her womb. Remember, He is omniscient!

Jesus Christ is the only one who can save us. Death had to occur for our bloodlines to be restored because the penalty of sin is death. Jesus, who was sinless, became sin to die for *all* sin.

[3] All praise to God, the Father of our Lord Jesus Christ. It is by his great mercy that we have been born again, because God raised Jesus Christ from the dead. Now we live with great expectation, [4] and we have a priceless inheritance—an inheritance that is kept in heaven for you, pure and undefiled, beyond the reach of change and decay.
—1 Peter 1:3–4 (ESV)

Jesus answered him, "Truly, truly, I say to you, unless one is born again he cannot see the kingdom of God."
—John 3:3 (ESV)

Earlier, I mentioned that Jesus died so that we would have the *opportunity* to have eternal life. God gives us free will. Whether we accept or reject that chance is up to us. We have the option to go from death to life. If you want to accept God's opportunity of eternal life, I urge you to take the first step of accepting God as your Savior by lifting your hands, which is the universal sign of surrender, and pray this prayer:

Dear God,
I know You love me. I believe You died and rose from the dead for my sins. Please forgive me for my sins. You are the only One that can save me. I invite you now into my life. I give you my heart and soul. Please be my Savior and Lord. Transform me and align me with Your will. Thank you for Your faithfulness and Your Love.
It is in Jesus's name I pray.
Amen.

Now that you have prayed this prayer and have invited God into your life, you are saved! The next step is transformation. It does not happen overnight, but it is necessary and rewarding. It is what sets us free! We can be saved but still be in bondage. I was saved at the age of seven, but I was in spiritual bondage until I was thirty-seven. The transformation step is the death of the old you and the rebirth of the new you in Christ Jesus. This involves aligning your will or desires with God's Will and aligning your lifestyle according to God's Word. It sounds overwhelming, but we will take it step by step. One of the first things we must know as Christians is what God says about us and how He defines us so that we can align our description of ourselves with His.

Before we begin, let's pray this prayer asking God to transform and manifest in our lives.

My Heavenly Father,

Thank You for loving me right where I am. I have given You my life, past, present, and future, and I have accepted You as my Lord and Savior. Transform and renew me. Align me with Your Word. Change my will to match Yours. Please manifest in my life. I thank You in advance for the works You will do through me.

It is in Jesus's name I pray.

Amen.

WHO DOES GOD SAY I AM?

irstly, I pose the question, "Who do you think you are?" Have you ever thought about it? It is an important question to know. Your definition of yourself correlates with the path you decide to take and help dictate your decisions in your life. So who do you think you are?

Activity #6

Answer the question, "Who do you think you are?" Briefly notate how you define yourself below.

_____

_____

_____

_____

_____

_____

Notice I did not ask about what you do for a living, what your name is, what roles you have taken on, what you like doing for hobbies, how you describe your attributes, or your gender, ethnicity, and socioeconomic background.

Did your answer involve any of these questions? Thankfully, who we are has nothing to do with any of these limiting aspects of our lives. Dr. Myles Munroe once stated, "To know who you are you must look at the source of life and not life itself."

Genesis chapter 1 states that God created light, the sky, land, seas, vegetation, trees, the sun, moon, stars, and animals by speaking them into existence. All these things came from the earth, the dirt. Nine out of thirty-one verses in this book and chapter began with "God said." However, when God created mankind, He did not just speak us into existence from dirt. God gave us His Spirit. Yes, He created the physical body from the earth, but it is only so we can operate here on Earth. So we are more than just a body—we are a spirit (God's Spirit) in a "dirt" body to fulfill a purpose on earth. We are not only created by God; we are of God. So we are children of the Most High God, heirs and heiresses of this earth.

———◆-◇-◆———

26 Then God said, "Let us make mankind in our image, in our likeness, so that they may rule over the fish in the sea and the birds in the sky, over the livestock and all the wild animals, and over all the creatures that move along the ground."
27 So God created mankind in his own image, in the image of God he created them; male and female he created them.
—Genesis 1:26–27 (NIV)

———◆-◇-◆———

The Word of God says that we are fearfully and wonderfully made (Ps. 139:13–16, NKJV). Let's look at the words "fearfully" and "wonderfully" for a moment. The dictionary definitions are as follows:

> **Fearfully** – *With extreme care and concern*
> **Wonderfully** – *In a way that inspires delight or admiration; extremely well*

What does this tell you?

You were made with extreme care and concern in a way that inspires joy and admiration.

You were not an accident, nor were you a mistake because God does not make mistakes or have accidents. Remember, He is omniscient and omnipotent. Do you know the meticulous process that occurred to make you? Your mother did not just carry you for about nine months and give birth to you. No. That *one* sperm, unique to you, out of about *100 million* sperm, fertilized your mother's egg at a fertile moment. Even a specific time and temperature may have had an effect. Then that embryo, the future you, had to transform, grow, and survive in the uterus of your mother. About 50 percent of embryos do not make it, but you did. God kept you and your mother safe throughout the entire incubation and birthing process, just as He is keeping you now. God gave you His likeness and placed His Spirit in you. None of this was by mistake or happenstance. You are here to bring glory to God's name by solving a problem, answering a question, or adding a contribution that will help transform this world for the better. God specifically created you for a distinct purpose that was determined before your existence, which means that you are precious. Therefore, it is important to know who you are so that you cannot be swayed when opposition comes.

*For I know the plans I have for you," declares the Lord, "plans to prosper
you and not to harm you, plans to give you hope and a future.*
—Jeremiah 29:11 (NIV)

This battle is not physical or of this world; it is a spiritual warfare. Actually, it is not even our battle! God has already won the war, which makes us conquerors when we accept God as our Lord and Savior. The devil's main goal is to infiltrate and control our thoughts. If the enemy can control our thoughts, he can ultimately control and imprison us by planting lies about our identity, what God has for us, and our purpose. The devil already knows our identities. The enemy knows he cannot take anything God has given us, including our identity. Instead, he seeks to preoccupy and tire us out in hopes of deterring us from reaching the plans God has for us.

*The thief does not come except to steal, and to kill, and to destroy. I have come
that they may have life, and that they may have it more abundantly.*
—John 10:10 (KJV)

*For we wrestle not against flesh and blood, but against principalities, against powers, against
the rulers of the darkness of this world, against spiritual wickedness in high places.*
—Ephesians 6:12 (KJV)

My daughter liked rainbows when she was younger. She would draw them in her art, wear colorful clothes to resemble the rainbow, stick rainbow stickers everywhere, and watch for the appearance of rainbows when it rained. One day, she was around a group of teenage cousins that were talking about the rainbow symbol and her stickers. They said that the rainbow was a symbol of homosexuality and that it should not be displayed unless an individual is gay or homosexual. My daughter, who has autism and was seven years old at that time, confidently, yet peaceably, replied, "No, a rainbow is God's promise that He will never flood the earth again. It's in Genesis, look it up." Then she walked away, melodically chanting, "I like rainbows." The teenagers were at a loss for words and did not bring it up again.

I tell this story to say this: Knowing brings confidence, which disarms lies, half-truths, and uncertainty. In order to stop the devil's infiltration, we must know God, know who we are in Him, and know what He says about us. So this next section is all about our identity and what God says about us.

The bottom line is that we were made in God's image to reflect and express His glory. We were created to rule over the earth according to God's Will and instructions and coexist in a community with one another in Love. (Remember, God is Love and Love is an action.) As Christians, we are to have a relationship with God, utilize our complete access to spiritual blessings from heaven to glorify Him and destroy the devil's endeavors by operating within and declaring the kingdom of God.

The devil wants to cloud our thoughts. For example, I used to have the following thoughts regularly:

1. When I began praying more: *You're praying and asking God for too much; dial it back.*
2. When I prayed about a difficult situation: *Why are you praying about this? You should just be thankful you're alive. What more do you want?*
3. *You don't deserve to have …* (Varied)
4. *You're not good enough to …* (Varied)
5. *Why would anyone or anything ever love someone like you? You're a mess!*

But the truth is:

Counter1. The Word of God tells me not to worry about anything; Pray about everything (Phil. 4:6–7, NKJV).

Counter2. In difficult times, the Word of God says to cast my burdens on Him, and He will sustain me (Ps. 55:22, NKJV).

Counter3. When I feel powerless and undeserving: God says that I have been strengthened with all power according to His glory and that I am His heir (Col. 1:11–13, NKJV)

Counter4. When I'm wrestling with feelings of worthlessness and low self-worth, and feel that I don't deserve things: God tells me that *all* have sinned and fallen short of His glory, but we are made righteous and worthy through the redemption of Jesus Christ (Rom. 3:23–25, NKJV).

Counter5. When I'm feeling that no one could ever love me: The Word of God says that He loves me so much that He gave His only begotten son to die for me (John 3:16, NKJV).

It is so important to hold every thought captive—meaning, we must dismiss things that are not of God while dwelling on the thoughts that are of God. Again, we must know what the Word of God says. Since we are created in God's image, we have the capacity to have the mindset of God. So anything outside of the mind or Will of God is unnatural and must be brought to the conformity of His Word. It takes discipline, but we must align ourselves with God. This includes our thoughts.

We know that anyone born of God does not continue to sin; the One who was born of God keeps them safe, and the evil one cannot harm them.
—1 John 5:18 (NIV)

In your relationships with one another, have the same mindset as Christ Jesus:
—Philippians 2:5 (NIV)

I was depressed for years. Ungodly thoughts constantly entered my mind, and I allowed it to redefine who I was to the point where I was completely confused about my purpose in life. Soon, I didn't see any reason why I should live. I believed that I had served my purpose of bringing my daughter into this world. I took several attempts on my life. I am thankful for my loving, omnipresent, omnipotent, omniscient God interceding for me when I could not do it on my own. Each time, either something drastic would occur to stop me or I would survive the detriment that I caused. Joyce Myers explained what she does when she has negative or ungodly thoughts in her head. She immediately speaks against it out loud and counteracts it with scripture (Meyers, 2020). So I tried it and have been doing it ever since. When those ungodly thoughts creep into my mind about my identity and capabilities, I speak against them immediately with what God says about me. It was awkward at first, but now it is second nature, and those thoughts occur less and less. Now, I find myself thinking godly thoughts, which have resulted in a more productive and fulfilling life. My mental and physical health has drastically improved, my spirit is lifted, I have joy and peace, my relationships with family and friends have improved, and I have become a better mother, daughter, sister, friend, etc. I've overcome the thoughts the devil puts in my head in an attempt to rattle me because the God that dwells in me is far greater than the enemy in the world.

I like the television show *Mom*. It is about a single mother who, after dealing with her battle with alcoholism and drug abuse, decides to restart her life in Napa, California, working as a waitress and attending Alcoholics Anonymous (AA) meetings with her mother, who is also a recovering addict. During their AA meeting shares, they begin by saying, "My name is … and I'm an alcoholic." I believe this is also the process for real-life AA meetings. One thing I never got was why they still labeled themselves as an alcoholic after being sober for so long.

We demolish arguments and every pretension that sets itself up against the knowledge of God, and we take captive every thought to make it obedient to Christ.
—2 Corinthians 10:5 (NIV)

⁴ You, dear children, are from God and have overcome them, because the one who is in you is greater than the one who is in the world. ⁵ They are from the world and therefore speak from the viewpoint of the world, and the world listens to them. ⁶ We are from God, and whoever knows God listens to us; but whoever is not from God does not listen to us. This is how we recognize the Spirit of truth and the spirit of falsehood.
—1 John 4:4–6 (NIV)

I am who God says I am. The devil wants us to identify with our ugly past to keep us stuck in that identity. God has deemed us as His children. So do not take on the wrong name. We are saved, delivered, redeemed, loved, healed, cherished, and restored. I know what it is like to have had things happen to you, things you have done, and bad things in your life playing on loop, over and over in your head. Believe me, I know what it's like. I had the same bad things play in my head on repeat for years. The devil wants to keep reminding us of these things so that we can dwell on them until it infects our spirit and breaks us down to a point where life is too unbearable to live.

Activity #7a

As we have discussed, the devil will try to redefine who we are to keep us in spiritual bondage and away from our purpose. What are some ungodly or negative thoughts about yourself that have plagued your mind? List at least three below.

1. _____

2. _____

3. _____

4. _____

5. _____

Activity #7b

Now look up what God says about you to counteract the thoughts you listed above. You can utilize the scriptures we have discussed, the Bible (printed copy or digital), or the scriptures throughout this workbook. Be sure to notate the book, chapter, and verse(s) so that you can reference it as needed. (For example, John 3:16)

Counter1. _____

_____

_____

Counter2. _____

_____

_____

Counter3. _____

_____

_____

Counter4. _____

_____

_____

Counter5. _____

_____

_____

Activity #7c: Try It Out

When I began countering the negative thoughts in my head, I found it beneficial to write down (verbatim or paraphrased) the scriptures on index cards where they were accessible to my eyes in passing at home. I also made copies to keep with me. I would read the cards aloud at least five times a day until I had them memorized. Perhaps this will work for you. Take this idea, alter it, and make it your own.

You could also try these options:

- Type it up, print it out, and post it in various places in your home.
- Record-and-Play—voice record it on your phone to play every day.
- Text it on your phone to your notes to read every day.

So why is it so important to know who you are in God?

It is important to know who God is and who God says you are so that you will never name yourself something that you're not. Knowing this helps safeguard you from underestimating what God can do *in* you and *through* you. It is so you will never let your fear belittle you, and thus, belittle God.

Let's pull an example from the Word of God. In Numbers chapters 13 and 14, God promised to give the Israelites Canaan, a land flowing with milk and honey. So scouts were sent out to bring back a report. Most of the scouts came back from Canaan with the report that they looked like grasshoppers to the people of Canaan. They put their insecurities and how they felt in comparison to the Canaanites in the Canaanites' mouths. The Bible doesn't say that the Canaanite people called them grasshoppers. They called themselves grasshoppers, an insect that can be unnoticeably stepped on as it blends in with the grass.

However, I do find it ironic that they used grasshoppers as the analogy. Caleb and Joshua made the statement that the Canaanites would not devour them, that the Israelite people would devour them. Similarly, despite their size, grasshoppers can devour large sums of plants. In fact, they benefit the ecosystem and have a significant influence on what types of plants grow from the ground. So insignificant due to size? I think not.

²⁷ They gave Moses this account: "We went into the land to which you sent us, and it does flow with milk and honey! Here is its fruit. ²⁸ But the people who live there are powerful, and the cities are fortified and very large. We even saw descendants of Anak there. ²⁹ The Amalekites live in the Negev; the Hittites, Jebusites and Amorites live in the hill country; and the Canaanites live near the sea and along the Jordan."
³⁰ Then Caleb silenced the people before Moses and said, "We should go up and take possession of the land, for we can certainly do it."
³¹ But the men who had gone up with him said, "We can't attack those people; they are stronger than we are." ³² And they spread among the Israelites a bad report about the land they had explored. They said, "The land we explored devours those living in it. All the people we saw there are of great size. ³³ We saw the Nephilim there (the descendants of Anak come from the Nephilim). We seemed like grasshoppers in our own eyes, and we looked the same to them."
—Numbers 13:27–33 (NIV)

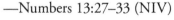

Furthermore, God went to great lengths to offer us salvation. So to say that you are insignificant is disrespectful to God, given that He placed his Spirit in you, created you in His likeness, and calls you His child. Then He went even further and made provisions through Jesus Christ to cover any sin that you may commit through the entire span of your life, all so you can have a right relationship with Him.

I managed a movie store when I was younger, and I am a huge movie buff. One of my favorite sagas is *Transformers*. Optimus Prime, the leader of the Autobots, constantly expresses who he is in every movie, especially in battle. Particularly, toward the end of the latest movie, *Transformers: The Last Knight*, Optimus arrives at the height of the battle in a grand fashion and defeats the Decepticons with ease. But before he does this, he states, "Did you forget who I am? I am Optimus Prime!" We need to get in the same mindset as Optimus and tell the enemy, with authority, who we are. "Devil, you must have forgotten who I am! I am a child of the Most High God, created in His image and likeness, and you have no authority over me!" Tell the enemy who you are!

ACKNOWLEDGE AND ADDRESS YOUR PAIN

We are no stranger to pain, physical or mental suffering, and trouble, as they are tied to sin since the fall of Adam. The word "pain" derives from the Latin word *pena*, which means penalty. It is a part of life whether we acknowledge it or not. What are you going to do with that pain? Adversity produces advancement. Your pain should advance you into your purpose. The only one that can turn your pain and all the bad that has happened in your life into good that advances you to your purpose is God. So do not hate the thing that brings you to the feet of God because that is the best place to be.

The goal is not to ignore our pain and struggles. It is not even to be delivered from it. Sometimes, it may be for us to endure trials because our answer, our blessing, is on the other side. It is through trials that God's greatness manifests, His glory is revealed, and the totality of our blessings is fulfilled. Therefore, the goal is to grow through and overcome them, but we must acknowledge them. The sooner we acknowledge it, the sooner we can turn it over to God and begin healing.

I will use a literal example to explain. I was a dancer for eighteen years. We were practicing for a partner performance for a major event. Ten days before the big day, my partner threw me in the air and dropped me on the concrete floor. I landed on one knee. The knee instantly swelled. I attempted to ignore the pain and walk it off, but the entire knee was bruised. Still, I denied I was in pain because the show must go on and I wanted to be in it. I bandaged it up and wore pants to cover it. At practice, people asked me about it, and I would quickly assure them that I was fine. "Just a little stiff, nothing major," I would say. I did not tell anyone I was in pain. I denied it so much that I began to believe I was okay. The bruising had turned purple and had begun to spread to behind and above the knee. Friends and family came to see the performance, and I performed with all I had at the event.

Afterward, everyone praised my performance. I looked over at my mother, and she was frowning and near tears. She walked over to me and tightly embraced me as she whispered, "I know you're in pain. Let's go and get you taken care of." She already knew without me saying a word. She sensed it.

So I finally acknowledged it and allowed her to care for me. It turns out, I had a fractured kneecap with severe swelling and bruising underneath. I have trouble with that knee now, fifteen years later, all because I did not acknowledge and address what happened to me.

In the same way, mental and emotional pain is real and can cause detriment in our lives if it goes unchecked. Our emotions are like a thermostat: they indicate what is going on with us physically, mentally, and spiritually (DeRamus, 2017). For example, I ignored my mental pain caused by the betrayal in my marriage and trouble at work for years. I just placed bandages on the situations I encountered because I did not want to face reality. My husband and I had a fairy-tale story, from how we met in high school to the wedding. It was like something out of a movie, and I did not want to let that go. I would brag and tell our story to anyone who wanted to hear it, even when the marriage was in shambles. The reality was that the marriage began to fall apart a few weeks before the wedding because we brought in unresolved pain and issues from our history and background that were not addressed. That pain only built until everything in nearly every aspect of our lives spiraled out of control. I internalized issues at the workplace until I became bitter, which negatively affected my productivity.

Comparison is the ultimate crippling tool of the devil. Well, at least it was the tool that crippled me for years. I used to constantly compare myself to images that people portrayed. The thing I failed to realize is that I saw only the highlight reel of people's lives. I would compare my shortcomings and low points to the successes that they publicly broadcast. Everyone seemed more successful, happier, more attractive, and just overall better people than I was. Even though I made a decent living, there were times I was ashamed of my job. I would try to avoid classmates and alienated myself from my family because I was so embarrassed that I did not have a higher-paying, more prestigious career. For a brief period, I compromised my beliefs and tried to change who I was to appeal more to my husband. I would constantly compare myself to others and deemed myself as less of a woman because I had seemingly failed at being a good wife. Soon my pain and struggles paralyzed me to the point that I was stagnant. I was just here. Lost and unfruitful, I could barely conduct the basic tasks of life.

Can you relate to any of these examples? The situations may not be exactly the same, but the failure to acknowledge pain and address issues that have occurred in the past or are currently occurring may be somewhat similar. In my story of physical pain, my mother sensed that I was in pain because of our connection. Once I acknowledged my pain and allowed her to help me, the healing process began. This act in this story was a human mother. God is significantly more capable of caring for us. Again, He created us in His likeness and gave us His Spirit, which deeply connects us to Him. God gives us free will to make our own decisions. He knows our pain and struggles and is right there waiting for us to acknowledge and call on Him to step into our situation because we cannot do it without Him.

If you, then, though you are evil, know how to give good gifts to your children, how much more will your Father in heaven give good gifts to those who ask him!
—Matthew 7:11 (NIV)

In the story of mental and emotional pain, I held on to a past that I viewed as worthy of a fairytale. Sometimes we can be in a state of such denial that we create fantasies to avoid addressing our reality. Comparison spawns the need to portray certain images to compete with others. We get so caught up on images, how something looks or appears, that we put on this front to give the impression that we have it all figured out. Meanwhile, that pain festers on the inside and chips away at our mental and spiritual wholeness. The more we deny our pain, troubles, and struggles, the worse they get, and the harder it gets to address them.

Oh, don't worry; we wouldn't dare say that we are as wonderful as these other men who tell you how important they are! But they are only comparing themselves with each other, using themselves as the standard of measurement. How ignorant!
—2 Corinthians 10:12 (NLT)

Am I now trying to win the approval of human beings, or of God? Or am I trying to please people? If I were still trying to please people, I would not be a servant of Christ.
—Galatians 1:10 (NIV)

Our pain is not a sin. We are human. So there is nothing to be ashamed of. Our pain and struggles are not what define us because they are temporary. We are all in bodies that are decaying as we speak. The devil, our enemy, wants us to suffer alone, and in silence. He wants us to himself so that he can eventually kill us. Think about it. When we are depressed, we usually isolate ourselves from others and lose interest in activities. We begin to dwell on that pain, and it breaks our spirit and steals our hope, which is why we need to go to the Source. This may lead to substance, sexual, or alcohol addiction, or other vices to numb the pain. The longer we remain in that depressive state, the deeper we go. We feel more pain, more heartache, more turmoil until we are numb and become completely paralyzed by our struggles. Have you ever smashed your finger or broken a bone? It is extremely painful. However, after a while, that pain turns to numbness and immobilization. Every so often, the range of motion is lost even after it has healed. *Pain. Numbness. Paralysis. Death.* It is what the enemy wants for us because we were each created for a unique purpose. God placed that purpose inside us. We feel it. If the enemy can keep you isolated and paralyzed by your pain, it keeps you weakened, thus increasing his chances of convincing you that you have no reason to live.

Remember our previous discussion about who God says we are. You are not doomed; you have a purpose. Every sin is forgivable to God. Suicide is a permanent solution to a temporary problem. It will never be the answer. Taking your life does not solve your problems. It causes more problems and pain for the loved ones you leave behind. God does not want you to take your life. He has a specific plan for you. So there is something inside of you that this world needs. Again, pain or grief is not a sin, nor is it an excuse to sin. We were created to worship and bring God glory by fulfilling our unique purpose.

In the next activity, I want you to think about your pain, sufferings, troubles, and struggles. The pain and problems are still there whether or not we try to forget them because they have not been addressed. Notice I did not say dwell on it. Thinking about something and dwelling on something are two different acts. We think about something to gain knowledge or logic about it. When we dwell on things, we stay and live in them. It becomes your home. For example, your residence is your dwelling place. We are to dwell in the house of the Lord, instead of our pain and struggles. Read the scriptures below.

—————⟫•◦•⟪—————

⁶ Surely goodness and mercy shall follow me all the days of my life:
and I will dwell in the house of the Lord for ever.
—Psalm 23:6 (KJV)

³ He restoreth my soul: he leadeth me in the paths of righteousness for his name's sake.
—Psalm 23:3 (KJV)

—————⟫•◦•⟪—————

What did you gather from the above scriptures? What is David saying here? Let's break this down. Verse 3 states that God restores David's soul and leads him on the paths of righteousness. The term "restore" in this instance means to rehabilitate or repair. Our soul is comprised of our heart and mind. We will learn more about the importance and composition of our soul later in the text. Then he goes on to say that God leads him on the paths of righteousness. In other words, God keeps him on the right path. That right there would be enough for me. However, David goes on to give more detail about what is included in the house of the Lord. After reading both scriptures, what and who are in the house of the Lord other than David? Well, if it is the house of the Lord, God is there. The very first word of the sixth verse should have gotten your attention. The word "surely" can translate to "without question" or "definitely." So whatever is to follow is a done deal.

We have discussed the word "dwell." David says, "I will dwell in the house of the Lord for ever." In addition, David adds that goodness and mercy will follow him.

So what can we conclude? If we dwell in the house of the Lord instead of in our pains, struggles, or flesh, our hearts will be restored. We will be led and shielded by God in front and shadowed by His goodness and mercy from behind. That should give you confidence, reassurance, and motivation to remain in God's presence no matter what! Let me give you a quick simile. Think of God and His goodness and mercy as bodyguards. Have you ever seen a celebrity or a famous public figure out in public? What do they always have standing around them? They have bodyguards ready to cover them at a moment's notice if needed. The public figure is led by a bodyguard in front to ensure that he/she remains on the path that the bodyguard has already covered. God does that same thing for us. When we dwell in His house or remain in His presence, He guides our paths. The bodyguards at the rear are to protect what he/she cannot see because the rear is a vulnerable state. That goodness and mercy does the same thing. It encompasses and compensates for unforeseen circumstances when we stumble off God's path in our lives.

Acknowledging our pain is the first step. Then putting it up front and center to lay it at God's feet is the next. The most important thing is that when you lay it at God's feet, you leave it there and release it. The best illustration I have seen of this was in a sermon by Preacher Jeremy Foster from Hope City Church. He used luggage to symbolize pain. Each piece of luggage was a different pain, struggle, or bad experience of the past. He carried about ten sizable pieces of luggage around and led with it everywhere he went. This was to depict that we tend to lead with our struggles. Here are some examples:

"This was done to me as a child. *So* I can never have a healthy relationship."

"My parents were alcoholics and were abusive toward me. *So* I do the same to my children."

"The love of my life divorced me. *So* I can never trust again."

If we lead in life with that baggage, we cannot elevate ourselves to where God wants us to go because we are weighed down by our pain and circumstances. Therefore, leave it with God because He is far greater than any pain, problem, or circumstance we could ever face. He will see you through it. Remember, He never leaves or forsakes us and His ways are *always* good.

12 Therefore, since we are surrounded by such a huge crowd of witnesses to the life of faith, let us strip off every weight that slows us down, especially the sin that so easily trips us up. And let us run with endurance the race God has set before us. ² We do this by keeping our eyes on Jesus, the champion who initiates and perfects our faith Because of the joy awaiting him, he endured the cross, disregarding its shame. Now he is seated in the place of honor beside God's throne.

—Hebrews 12:1–2 (NLT)

We hold on to things for sentimental reasons. Other times, we hold on to things simply because we believe that we need them. Sometimes, we have no idea why we hold on to certain things. I'll give you a practical example, but no judging! I am a sentimental hoarder. Up until about three years ago, I still had my work from school, kindergarten through college. I was a dancer for about eighteen years. The key word here is "*was*" a dancer. I still have every dance shoe, leotard, and costume I have ever danced and performed in. I kept hospital bracelets! Yes, the bands that the hospital places around your arm with your identity and date of admission. I kept those. In all fairness, my mother started it, but there is no excuse for why I continued it and took it to a new level! As the years passed, more things accumulated. I bought my first house and carried it all from my mother's house to my new home. I got married and accumulated more stuff. Most of it ended up in the attic. I had a daughter and continued the cycle. I even voluntarily kept some of my husband's things in case he needed or wanted them, (By the way, he had no idea I was keeping them and did not want any of them.) God blessed us with the very home that my husband used to dream of owning as a child. Do you know how difficult it was to transport all of that "stuff" into our new home?

Our first home was a smaller home. We did not appear to have many things. It was nice and organized. So we had no problem getting volunteers to help us. Everyone thought the same thing. *This would take about a day to pack, load, move and unpack.* However, they did not see the unseen, the hidden things in the attic and the closets. Even with eight people, it took about a week to move our things into the new home solely because of the excess "stuff" in those hidden areas I had accumulated! Needless to say, they did not help us unpack everything as they had their own lives to live. It took me about six months to unpack and stash things away again. After seven years, half of the items are still in crates! Every so often, when I have conserved some energy and have some time, I clean out a crate or two. I give it a final look, reminisce, and throw it away. If I am honest, I have come across some things I don't know why I kept. Crazy, right? Well, holding on to and carrying our pain and insecurities also impairs and delays movement in our lives. It is deadweight. We can look good and appear to have it all together on the outside but be harboring some terrible, traumatic things inside our hearts and mind, just as in my example of things hidden in the closets and attic. Again, our pain is not a sin. However, the pain of your past should be just that—your past. Strive to live that way. Your future is not ahead of you, it is within you, but it is trapped by the hoarding of pain and insecurities. Release it to God, our omnipresent, omniscient, omnipotent, and Sovereign Father in Heaven!

²⁹ Take My yoke upon you and learn from Me [following Me as My disciple], for I am gentle and humble in heart, and you will find rest (renewal, blessed quiet) for your souls. ³⁰ For My yoke is easy [to bear] and My burden is light."
—Matthew 11:29–30 (AMP)

The Bible declares that we are to get rid of anything that slows us down from doing what God has intended for us to do, *including* sin. So this means that sin will not be the only thing distracting us from fulfilling the purpose that God has for us. Experiencing pain, suffering, and anger are not sins, but they can deter us from a life of abundance if we allow them to do so. In addition, doing good things in your life and doing the right thing for your life are not the same things. Meaning, we can get busy doing things in life that are not bad, but that is distracting us from operating in our purpose. Read the scripture below.

12 So we have many people of faith around us. Their lives tell us what faith means. So let us run the race that is before us and never give up. We should remove from our lives anything that would get in the way. And we should remove the sin that so easily catches us. ² Let us look only to Jesus. He is the one who began our faith, and he makes our faith perfect. Jesus suffered death on the cross. But he accepted the shame of the cross as if it were nothing. He did this because of the joy that God put before him. And now he is sitting at the right side of God's throne.
—Hebrews 12:1–2 (ICB)

Activity #8

What has you in pain? What have you been carrying around with you? What is overwhelming you? Were there things done to you in your past that you cannot seem to forgive or overcome? Are there things now that are crippling you and preventing you from stepping into your purpose and accepting the blessings that God has for you? Have you done things that you cannot forgive yourself for? Number and list everything below. We are going to acknowledge it and give it to God so that you can be free of it once and for all!

_____

_____

_____

_____

_____

_____

_____

_____
_____
_____
_____
_____
_____
_____
_____
_____
_____
_____
_____
_____
_____

No matter the circumstances, I can assure you that God has blessed you and made you stronger than your problems. He told us that we will have struggles but gave us comfort in knowing that He has already overcome the world. So give praise to God because your victory is secured.

Activity #9

How many problems did you list in the previous activity? List at least as many things that you can thank and worship God for below. For example, if you listed eight things you are suffering from in the previous activity, list at least eight things for which you can thank and worship God.

_____
_____
_____
_____
_____
_____
_____
_____
_____
_____
_____

When we are in physical pain, like a broken limb, we go to a physician, a doctor. When we are depressed or have anxiety, we may see a psychiatrist or a counselor. However, psychiatrists can only do so much. A psychiatrist is good for helping us cope with our current state. What about becoming *whole* and solidifying an abundant future? A psychiatrist can diagnose our mental illness and help us cope, and a counselor can guide us to deal with our pain and regrets. What about being completely delivered from the root of addictions, vices, depression, pain, and regrets from the past? What about saving and restoring our souls?

Let me give you a practical depiction of this. I live near a large reservoir in a wooded area. We often find snakes and rodents hiding in our bushes. One day, my husband told the lawn man to cut our bushes down to lessen the chance of housing these "unwanted guests." I was furious when I came home from work to find that my rosebushes had been completely cut down. I made such a fuss about it. Imagine my surprise a few months later when those rosebushes resurfaced fuller and more vibrant than before. The lawn man had cut only what he could see on the surface. He did not remove the roots, the source of its growth. He can mow over it or cut it down, but if the root is intact under the surface, it can still resurface. Similarly, the root must be addressed in overcoming pain, addiction, vices, and other struggles we may face. If not, it can resurface.

Let me be clear: I have nothing against psychiatrists and counseling. In fact, I have had counseling and it is highly beneficial. They provide treatment to patients. The root word "treat" derives from the Latin word *tracture*, which means handle, deal with, or negotiate (*Online Etymology Dictionary*, 2021). Treatment and coping are different from being made whole and healed. My point is that God is our Source, our Creator. Psychiatrists and counselors are human beings like us, which means they have their own issues and make mistakes as well. They go to school to study theories and methods to administer treatment to patients to the best of their human ability. Go to counseling and seek treatment, yes. Absolutely. However, depend more on our Source. God is the answer. Dr. Anita Phillips is a renowned psychiatrist that combines faith with therapy. She said something that stuck with me. She said that all information from her college education, professional training, psychology, and theory books must be filtered through the Word of God before it becomes law for her (Phillips, 2020). She goes straight to the Source.

I get a kick out of installing, building, and programming things. I have installed chandeliers, dimmers for recessed lighting, floors, television stands, drafting tables, you name it. The more complex, the better. I especially enjoy programming new electronics and installing software. What does each of these items include? The manufacturer of every product includes a manual for the consumer to ensure that the product does what it was made to do and is utilized at its fullest potential. Manuals are important, which is why I have a designated drawer of them for nearly every product I purchase in case I need to refer to it to resolve issues or have operational questions. If the product does not perform correctly, is not installed properly, or is not fully utilized (for any reason), it reflects on the manufacturer. This is so important that most manufacturers, especially the more successful ones, have customer service and technical support departments for users. Furthermore, the manual is the manufacturer's instructions for the product, which we can either choose to follow or ignore.

¹⁶ All Scripture is inspired by God and is useful to teach us what is true and to make us realize what is wrong in our lives. It corrects us when we are wrong and teaches us to do what is right. ¹⁷ God uses it to prepare and equip his people to do every good work.
—2 Timothy 3:16–17 (NLT)

In the same way, we were created through Adam by God, our Manufacturer. Guess what. He left us a manual as well. It is called the Bible. The Bible tells us who we are and what we are to do here on earth. In addition, we have specialized "tech support," called the Holy Spirit, that constantly speaks to us, giving us guidance and support. I can go even farther and say that God uses other individuals, pastors, ministers, and mentors as customer service representatives to support us in our journey. Think back to God identifying Himself with a king. Do you remember what we discussed about a king's glory? Remember that we are the glory of God, which means that we are a reflection of Him, just as a product is a reflection of its manufacturer. Manufacturers place a warranty and a guarantee in the manual of every product created to assure its users that it has been tested and will fully operate to its potential. If it malfunctions, the operator or consumer can return it and either receive a new product or the repaired product. Similarly, we were tested before we were in our mother's womb. Otherwise, we would not be here on earth in the image of God. If you said the prayer and accepted Jesus Christ as your Lord and Savior, you have given yourself back to God, our manufacturer, and you have been restored and renewed! So live courageously in God's name because your success is in His best interest!

Activity #10a

Let's make the enemy tremble! We have discussed who God is, His Power, His Love for us, our authority, and His Will. So let's go back to your list of pain and struggle written for activity #8. Write them down again below. Only this time, write them in sentence form and add "BUT GOD!" in all caps at the end.

_____
_____
_____

Now let's break this down. The pain and struggles written in activity #8 are real, but your statement needed to be revised because it wasn't complete. A comma indicates a small break, which means you are not meant to stay where you are. When you place a comma and "but" behind your pain, it signifies that it is not over! The word "but" is a contradicting coordinating conjunction that negates or cancels out anything that comes before it. So anytime negative thoughts creep in your head or you are reminded of your pain, hold that thought captive and confidently revise the statement with a comma and "BUT GOD." In Exodus 3:14, God said, "I AM WHO I AM." Meaning, God is whatever you need Him to be and is able to do what you need Him to do and more. He is the Deliverer, Healer, Redeemer, Way Maker, Strength, Provider, and so much more. His name is Power, which is why "BUT GOD" is so befitting for every situation, issue, or struggle.

The name of the Lord is a strong tower; the righteous man runs into it and is safe.
—Proverbs 18:10 (ESV)

Activity #10b

In this scripture, the word "tower" in the Bible often refers to a literal tower, but in the above scripture, it is used figuratively as a symbol for protection and provision. Notice that just the Name of the Lord is not just a tower but a *Strong* Tower! Surely, you are safe! Now go back to activity #10a and read each *completed* statement out loud with the authority that God has given you! Take your freedom back!

I know that it will not be easy to just let it go. It will not be easy to just leave those cares at God's feet and trust that He's got you. God knows every struggle. Just as the above scripture describes, Jesus experienced not only the sins of the world, but also pain, shame, and death at the cross. However, He let it go because He knew that it was just temporary. Joy was ahead, and He would eventually be with God. We are to follow Jesus's example. Again, this is a process. You may have to read Activity #10a, the scriptures, and other sections several times before you believe it and allow it to become a part of you.

Pastor April Carter of Church of the Highlands depicts a great illustration of letting go in one of her messages. She tells the story of the monkey and the banana. Basically, a banana is placed in a mason jar (Carter, 2021). The monkey comes, reaches in to grab the banana, but cannot remove it from the jar. It sees its captors coming with nets but continues to frantically struggle to remove the banana from the jar. Similarly, bananas are placed inside a barred cage. The monkey would reach in and grab a banana but is unable to pull it out. In both instances, the monkey allowed itself to get captured. Questions: Why couldn't the monkey get the banana out of the jar or cage? What would the monkey have to have done to be free from the confinement jar or cage? Why did I say the monkey "allow" itself to get captured? Well, when you grip something, your hand makes a fist, which takes up more space. So the monkey's fist was too large to exit the mouth of the jar and the barred cage. On a side note, a closed fist rarely accomplishes anything. It rarely protects us or enriches us. All the monkey had to do was let go of the banana and he would have been freed from either confinement! Its fist could still open and close. It was the monkey's choice to hold on to the banana, which is why I said that he "allowed" itself to get captured. The transparency of the jar and the cage is what I like best about this analogy because it translates so well to how we can be with our pain, regrets, and insecurities. We see the enemy approaching to utilize our regrets to cripple us. We know that the enemy uses our pain and insecurities to throw us into a relentless cycle that deters us from our purpose. The enemy uses these things to weigh us down. Still, we will not let go of it. Other people around us are seeing it play out and wonder, "Why won't you just end that unhealthy or abusive relationship?," "Why don't you just forgive yourself and move on?" "Why would anyone think like that about themselves?," or "I don't see why you are insecure about something so small!" So make sure that you let it go. Let everything you listed in Activity #8a go and trust it with God. Remember, it is a process. Trust the process. It is easier said than done, but it is well worth it when you finally do it. I am a living witness.

Activity #11

Below is Isaiah 40:27–31. However, you will be personalizing it by replacing "Jacob" with your name and "Israel" with "son" or "daughter," whichever applies (Carter, 2021). Insert your information. Then, read it aloud and soak in every word. Read it as many times as you need!

[27] O _____, how can you say the Lord does not see your troubles?

(Insert Your Name)

O _____, how can you say God ignores your rights? [28] Have you never

(Insert "Son" or "Daughter")

heard? Have you never understood? The Lord is the everlasting God, the Creator of all the earth. He never grows weak or weary. No one can measure the depths of his understanding. [29] He gives power to the weak and strength to the powerless. [30] Even youths will become weak and tired, and young men will fall in exhaustion. [31] But those who trust in the Lord will find new strength. They will soar high on wings like eagles. They will run and not grow weary. They will walk and not faint.

Reflection

Give a summary of your thoughts on trusting in God, releasing your pain and struggles to Him, and starting your journey to spiritual freedom.

_____

_____

_____

_____

_____

_____

So what's next? After we acknowledge our pain, habits, and struggles and release it to God, the healing can begin! Releasing your problems to God means that you focus on Him and His greatness instead of anything you have going on around you. Healing will not happen overnight. Does an open wound completely heal overnight? A broken limb? What happens when you peel the scab off a wound? It bleeds again and is painful. It increases the risk of infection, and the wound must start the healing process again. The wound must be medicated, covered, and given the opportunity to heal. Similarly, our pains, habits, and struggles are like open wounds. If we continue to harbor on it and feed into the pain, it is like continuously peeling the scab off a wound. It too must be medicated, covered, and given the opportunity to heal. Acknowledging the pain and releasing it to God supplies the medication and coverage. However, giving yourself the opportunity to heal can be difficult to do because we can revert to that depressive, captured state, and delay the healing process. Therefore, it is so important to remember who God is and who we are in God to keep us on track.

Now let me give you a practical example of how God covers us. We would often visit my grandmother before she passed. She lived in an apartment complex. During one of our visits, she became agitated with one of her new young neighbors across from her as he would play loud music outside that everyone could hear. She said that the thumping of the music would often give her headaches. She and other neighbors filed a complaint, but the apartment manager did nothing about it. Well, this time, Granny Betty stepped outside her door and told him to turn the music down. The young man and his friend cussed at her, called her profane names, and threatened her. Granny Betty, four feet eleven and being my Granny Betty, did not back down. They continued to argue, and the young man and his friend stood up in an attempt to intimidate her as they did other neighbors. But what they did not expect was for her tall, behemoth of a grandson to silently stand behind her. He nearly took up the entire doorway! Those men sat back down, apologized, and turned the music down. They did not cause any trouble after that incident. Granny Betty never even saw her grandson behind her. He sat back down after he made his presence known, assuring those men that his Granny Betty was covered. In the same way, we may not see God with our physical eyes, but His presence is made known because we are His. So we are covered. The enemy, in the same way as those young men, backs away because he knows that when God is for us, no one, including him, can ever stand against us! With God, we are *more* than conquerors! Sometimes we forget that God is greater than any problem we could ever have in this world and that He will *never* forsake us because we are His children. We often tend to emphasize our problems instead of emphasizing God's greatness. We must magnify our God instead of magnifying our pain and problems. In the example, even though she had her grandson's support, Granny Betty argued back and forth with the neighbor herself, which increased her stress level and negative emotion. Likewise, we get flustered as we try to tackle our struggles on our own because we forget that we are not alone and are already covered. We just need to release it to Him and ask for help. Read the scripture below.

[31] What shall we say about such wonderful things as these? If God is for us, who can ever be against us? [32] Since he did not spare even his own Son but gave him up for us all, won't he also give us everything else? [33] Who dares accuse us whom God has chosen for his own? No one—for God himself has given us right standing with himself. [34] Who then will condemn us? No one—for Christ Jesus died for us and was raised to life for us, and he is sitting in the place of honor at God's right hand, pleading for us. [35] Can anything ever separate us from Christ's love? Does it mean he no longer loves us if we have trouble or calamity, or are persecuted, or hungry, or destitute, or in danger, or threatened with death? [36] (As the Scriptures say, "For your sake we are killed every day; we are being slaughtered like sheep.") [37] No, despite all these things, overwhelming victory is ours through Christ, who loved us.
—Romans 8:31–37 (NLT)

Now, pray the prayer below thanking God for releasing you from your pain and struggle. As you pray, concentrate on who we have discussed God is, His magnitude, and His reach instead of your current, temporary circumstances.

My Sovereign God and Heavenly Father,

You are omnipotent. You are all-powerful. There is absolutely nothing too hard for You. You are everywhere at the same time because You are omnipresent. You are always with me no matter where I am. And You are omniscient. You are all-knowing. You know my past, what's going on with me now, and what's to come in my future. Lord, You are bigger than any struggle I could ever face, and I find peace in knowing that You, MY FATHER, has already overcome the world, which makes me an overcomer! So I release all my pain and struggle right now and give it ALL to You because you said cast ALL my cares on You. You said in Your Word that Your yolk is easy, and Your burden is light. Thank You, Lord, for freeing me to live an abundant, purposeful life. Now that I have given it all to You, help me to leave it with you and move forward in thanksgiving, joy, and the authority you have given me as Your child.

It is in Jesus's Name I pray.

AMEN.

Acknowledging and addressing your past, pain, and struggles free you and set you up with a clean slate to begin a purposeful journey. As I stated earlier, I enjoy conducting installations. I consider myself a DIY enthusiast, as I also like remodeling and refinishing things. I remember my first remodel—the master bedroom of my first house. I wanted to make a bold statement. So I painted my bedroom walls a deep red with black molding. Later, I realized that it was a mistake. So I decided on a lighter, neutral color instead. As I painted the first wall, I realized that the red was bleeding through. I took a break to let it dry. The wall looked to be a reddish-orange because of the red underneath. I gave it a second coat. No luck. The red still came through. If you have any knowledge about painting, you know that I missed a significantly important step. There is this product called paint primer. A premium, multi-surface paint primer not only has excellent adhesion, but it can also cover and block heavy stains and imperfections, eliminate odors, provide mildew protection, and prepare the surface better for painting. Once I covered the red walls and black molding with a primer, the red and black did not bleed through. The new paint color was exactly as it was intended to look. Why am I talking about paint jobs? I realized I had made a mistake. I tried to do it with my methods of doing things but that red, my mistake, just kept bleeding through. In my method, I skipped a step. I was unsuccessful until I got something stronger than regular paint to cover the red. It is the same in life. No matter how hard we work, there are some things that only God can cover. Our human methods will not mend our spiritual brokenness and preserve our souls. So we cannot afford to skip out on a close relationship with God. You just acknowledged and addressed your pain and struggles by giving it all to God. So what you have done is primed over it all, just as I did on those red walls. God is the Primer. Just as paint primer is for multiple surfaces, God can prime any circumstance, pain, or struggle that we may have. He said that He is always with us; He will never leave us or forsake us, the ultimate adhesion. He covers all our imperfections and the stains of our past while eliminating foulness and providing protection from decay for our mind, spirit, and soul. Our past is still our past. It does not change what has been done or the pain we felt. It just doesn't bleed out. All that's left is beauty that exalts the glory of God. Soon you won't even remember how it looked or what life was like before the transformation. I see pictures of the red walls and wonder, *What was I thinking?* They were hideous! It is the same with life. In my life, I recall snapshots of who I was. People remind me, "I remember when …" It no longer bothers me because it gives me an opportunity to brag about God and how He changed my life. Gospel musician Travis Greene sings "There's more grace in Him than sin in me; Thank You for being God." There is no sin too great, no past too tainted, and no pain too severe for God to cleanse, heal, and restore. He has us covered. Omnipresent. Omniscient. Omnipotent.

PRAYER

Christianity is not the only religious faith that prays. Buddhism, Islam, Hinduism, Satanism, scientology, agnosticism, and any other religion or belief in the world pray, they just pray to and worship different things. The reason that all religions pray is because of who we are. Remember that we are a spirit (God's Spirit) inside of a dirt body. So it is in us to have a natural desire to connect to something on a spiritual level. Some people use Ouija boards, white magic, black magic, astrology, horoscopes, or even physical objects such as a statue or a structure. Of course, we will be discussing prayer to the omnipotent, omnipresent, omniscient King of all kings and Lord over all lords. God set eternity in our hearts to connect with Him. Prayer is an important key to God's kingdom. So we will discuss what prayer is and how God says we should pray.

10 I have seen the burden God has laid on the human race. 11 He has made everything beautiful in its time. He has also set eternity in the human heart; yet no one can fathom what God has done from beginning to end.
—Ecclesiastes 3:10–11 (NIV)

Remember, God gave us free will, dominion over the earth, and does not intervene unless we invite Him to do so. God will never break His promises, nor will He go against or circumvent what He has already said or done. So prayer is needed for God to intervene.

Have you ever noticed that children recite your words back to you? You must be mindful of what you say and promise a child because you will hear it again! For example, my daughter enjoys going to the arcade. I remember her asking her dad one Saturday morning to take her and her cousin to the arcade. She said, "Hey, Dad, can you please take my cousin and me to the arcade today?" Her dad was busy working from home but promised to take her next Friday after school if her grades were good. Although she was a little frustrated, she accepted it and looked forward to it. Thursday came along. In our conversation, she spoke about going to the arcade on Friday as if it was already a reality. Her dad thought that she would forget. She said, "You remember that you promised last Saturday that you would take me to the arcade after school on Friday if my grades were good. Here are my grades dad. They are all good. So that means you will bring me because you promised it." Her dad and I just looked at each other. Anyway, they had a great time at the arcade that Friday. Here is the point. The Word of God is full of promises—some with stipulations, some without. Prayer is the communication or petitioning of these promises. Let's break down this practical example. First, she acknowledged her dad as the authority and requested something that she knows he can provide. When he gave her an answer, she humbly accepted it and had faith that it would come to pass just as he had promised. Notice that his promise had a stipulation—good grades. She fulfilled that stipulation to align with his expectations and expected her request to be fulfilled based on his promise. Read the scripture below.

[14] *if my people, who are called by my name, will humble themselves and pray and seek my face and turn from their wicked ways, then I will hear from heaven, and I will forgive their sin and will heal their land.*
—2 Chronicles 7:14 (NIV)

What would have happened if she had not asked him to take her to the arcade? The chances of him taking her would have been slim because the request was not made. Her dad knows that she enjoys going to the arcade. It is not that her dad did not want to take her, she just did not make the request. Do you think he still would have taken her if she had failing grades? Well, no matter how much her dad wants to fulfill her request, if the stipulation was not met, then the request is null and void. It sounds similar to a courtroom or legal system, right? Well, praying to God is more of a petition than a religious act. Yes, a petition, like in the court system. Rituals, ceremonies, chants, and other religious traditions are not necessary for prayer. Collective prayer is good, but not necessary for God to hear you. It is communication between you and God. It is the acknowledgment of our need for Him as our Source and the petitioning of the promises that He has already made to us as it is our right as His children to do so. Those rights, along with principles and stipulations, are in the Bible, which is another reason we should study and meditate on it. The term petition means to make a formal request to an authority with respect to a particular cause. In the practical example of my daughter and her dad, she has rights to make requests and expect answers and fulfillment because she is his child, has a good relationship with him, and remains in alignment by meeting her dad's standards. Now she could still make requests solely because she is his child. It does not mean that her requests will be fulfilled. For example, if your child cussed you out, spit in your face, and requested two hundred dollars, would you be inclined to grant him/her that request? Well, I'll just speak for myself and answer … and that is a hard "No."

Similarly, we are children of the Most High God, our Source, and King of all kings. The omnipotent, omniscient, and omnipresent Ruler over all things created us by giving us His Spirit, a purpose, dominion over the earth, and privilege to call Him our Heavenly Father. This comes with rights!

18 About that time the disciples came to Jesus and asked, "Who is greatest in the Kingdom of Heaven?" 2 Jesus called a little child to him and put the child among them. 3 Then he said, "I tell you the truth, unless you turn from your sins and become like little children, you will never get into the Kingdom of Heaven. 4 So anyone who becomes as humble as this little child is the greatest in the Kingdom of Heaven.
—Matthew 18:1–4 (ESV)

Prayer can be defined as a necessary component of spirituality that permits heavenly intercession on earth (Munroe, 2018). Dr. Tony Evans, Oak Cliff Bible Fellowship pastor explains that prayer is relational communication with God for the purpose of making heaven visible on earth (Evans, *Prayer That Works*, 2019). Have you ever heard the Southwest Airlines slogan, "You are now free to move about the country"? Prayer is like a passport. It gives God access to do what He already wants to do for you. Some of those things have conditions attached to it, which is why we must pray and know the Word of God. The Bible declares in 1 Thessalonians 5:17 that we should pray without ceasing. It should be a constant. So we should be as familiar with prayer as we are with breathing.

The Bible gives us do's and don'ts, instructions, and examples of prayer. Read the scripture below and complete the activity.

5 "And when you pray, you must not be like the hypocrites. For they love to stand and pray in the synagogues and at the street corners, that they may be seen by others. Truly, I say to you, they have received their reward. 6 But when you pray, go into your room and shut the door and pray to your Father who is in secret. And your Father who sees in secret will reward you. 7 "And when you pray, do not heap up empty phrases as the Gentiles do, for they think that they will be heard for their many words. 8 Do not be like them, for your Father knows what you need before you ask him.
—Matthew 6:5–8 (ESV)

Activity #12

Answer the following questions by referencing Matthew 6:5–8. Circle "Yes" or "No."

1.	Do we need an audience to pray?	Yes	No
2.	Do others need to see or know that we are praying?	Yes	No
3.	Should intimate prayer be between you and God?	Yes	No
4.	Do we need to use graduate-level words when we pray?	Yes	No
5.	Is praying a mindless chant?	Yes	No
6.	Do our prayers have to be lengthy?	Yes	No
7.	Does God know what we need before we ask Him?	Yes	No
8.	Is prayer mandatory for the children of God?	Yes	No

Before we break down Matthew 6:9–13, we need to discuss the backstory of why Jesus is saying it. The Bible states that Jesus would wake up early before the day in the morning and go off by Himself to pray. Scholars say that morning in Israel began around 4:00 a.m. Jesus woke up before that. The markets did not open until about 8:00 a.m. That means that Jesus prayed for at least four hours every morning before most people even got out of bed. The disciples just used their logic. They noticed that Jesus would leave in the middle of the night to go and do something for hours. Then He would return, go out, and perform all these miracles. The disciples were with Him for most of the day. They witnessed, followed, and knew everything else Jesus had done throughout the day. However, prayer was the one thing Jesus habitually did. That was the difference, which is why they equated the miracles with what He did when He went away every single morning by Himself. *Pray.* Instead of asking, "Teach us to walk on water," "Teach us to cast out demons," "Teach us to raise someone from the dead," or "Teach us to heal the sick," the disciples asked Jesus, *"Teach us how to pray."* because they realized that the power to do miracles was somehow coming from prayer. This brings us to Matthew 6:9–13, where Jesus responds to their request.

35-37 While it was still night, way before dawn, he got up and went out to a secluded spot and prayed. Simon and those with him went looking for him. They found him and said, "Everybody's looking for you."
—Mark 1:35–37 (MSG)

Matthew 6:9–13, better known as The Lord's Prayer, is simply an example of how to pray. It was never meant to be repeated verbatim as an actual prayer. Look at the first four words of Matthew 6:9. It states, "Pray then *like this*," not "Pray this" or "Pray this prayer," which means use this as an example. Let's break each section down to uncover how God wants us to pray.

⁹ Pray then like this:
"Our Father in heaven,
hallowed be your name.
¹⁰ Your kingdom come,
your will be done,
on earth as it is in heaven.
¹¹ Give us this day our daily bread,
¹² and forgive us our debts,
as we also have forgiven our debtors.
¹³ And lead us not into temptation,
but deliver us from evil.
¹⁴ For if you forgive others their trespasses, your heavenly Father will also forgive you, ¹⁵ but if
you do not forgive others their trespasses, neither will your Father forgive your trespasses.
—Matthew 6:9–15 (ESV)

The first segment, "Our Father in Heaven" denotes quite a few things. It demonstrates that the very first thing you do in a prayer is acknowledge the relationship or connection you have with God. He is your Heavenly Father. But wait, there's more! It says, "*Our* Father in Heaven," which means that you are not an only child! This world does not revolve around any of us. We must share and support each other as brothers and sisters in Christ. Also, it displays the acknowledgment of God, just as in my practical example with my daughter and her dad.

The next line states "hallowed be your name." The term "hallow" derives from the Old English term *hālga*, which means "holy" or "sacred" (*Online Etymology Dictionary*, 2021). I believe that this part should serve as a reminder to us when we are going to God to pray. It reminds us that we are not just talking to anyone. For example, do you talk to your dad or the most highly respected people in your life in the same way as if they were children, strangers, or even friends? No, usually you will watch what you say and how you say it. Every now and then, my daughter will word something in an informal way with a "familiar" tone. When that happens, I immediately remind her by saying, "Who are you talking to?" She immediately apologizes and rewords her statement in a respectful tone.

Next, we must declare that His principles, the principles of the Kingdom of Heaven, applies to you here on earth ("Your kingdom come"). Furthermore, you want your will to align with God's Will, not the other way around ("Your will be done, on earth as it is in heaven"). This tells us that we should not be asking anything outside of the Will of God. This goes back to knowing God and studying His Word to know His Will.

The next portion, "Give us this day our daily bread," acknowledges that God is our Source in which we can live. Bread symbolizes multiple things in the Bible. Jesus said that He is the Bread of life in John 6:35. During the Lord's Supper, Jesus rationed the bread out to the disciples and said that it represented His body (1 Cor. 11:23–24, NKJV). Bread also symbolizes blessings from God. In Exodus 16:4, Moses fed His people in the desert with bread that fell from heaven. In these instances, it can also signify portioning overflow. He is our supply and help. Remember, we are all children of God. Again, the prayer example is including others by saying, "Give *us* this day *our* daily bread." Therefore, the overflow of God's blessing should not be accepted tightfisted. Keep in mind, a closed fist rarely benefits us. Instead, it traps us and prevents us from abundance. Others should be considered. God will give us what we need daily. Thus, we need not worry about holding on to today's bread/blessing overflow. God blesses us through one another. So the overflow should be shared or distributed to others. I mentioned earlier that the world does not revolve around any one of us and that we are not the only child God has. We are all connected through Christ. I'll give you a practical example of how blessings and overflow work. What happens when a child has siblings and is blessed with a toy, clothes, or other tangible items? Is that item only for that child, or does it pass through the other siblings, family, friends, or even strangers? I am the oldest granddaughter on my mom's side of the family. When I was about two years old, my great-grandmother bought me a mink coat. I was told that I loved wearing my coat. I even wanted to wear it in the summer. Soon I outgrew the coat. My mother took it to the cleaners once more and put it up until my aunt, her younger sister, had a baby girl. The coat was passed down to her to enjoy. She was followed by two sisters. Both little sisters enjoyed the coat as well. After her daughters outgrew the coat, my aunt took it to the cleaners to preserve it and returned it to me for my future daughters. A few years later, I became godmother to a friend's daughter. She wore the coat. My friend returned it to me some years later in time for my daughter to wear it as well. Like everyone who preceded her, she enjoyed wearing the coat. She wore it around the house all the time. Soon those sleeves began to crawl farther and farther up her arm. Once again, I preserved the coat and stored it until my cousin had her two daughters. It was cleaned, preserved, and returned to me about a year ago, and it awaits to be enjoyed again. That mink coat is in the same condition as it was in when I wore it over thirty years ago. Blessings are never meant to just be held on to. God blesses us for His Name's sake and His glory. So we must share our blessings and the overflow of our daily bread.

Why not ask for our weekly bread, monthly bread, or even yearly bread? That would surely save time, right? Well, asking God to give us our daily bread means that we go to Him the next day and ask for our daily bread again, which keeps us in fellowship with God. He wants a close relationship with each of us. Plus, what do you think would happen if we asked for our yearly bread? Remember, God assured us that we will have trouble in this life on earth. God will never give us a life that makes Him unnecessary. If we were to sporadically go to Him to get advances on our "daily bread," we would get into so much trouble managing things on our own! As stated earlier, "bread" symbolizes God or blessings from God. He knows what's best for us. He knows how much to give us because He knows what we can handle. Even though we are children of the Most High God, He is the Omniscient, Omnipresent, and Omnipotent One, not us. So we would surely stumble and dig ourselves a deep hole if He gave us long-term portions all at once.

The next section is "And forgive us for our trespasses, as we forgive them that trespass against us." (Matthew 6:12 (NMB)). The term "trespass" derives from the Latin word *transpassare*, which translates to "to pass over" (Online Etymology Dictionary, 2021). Another meaning of this translation would be to disregard, disrespect, or sin. Forgiveness is so important that it is emphasized again after the example prayer in the fourteenth and fifteenth verses. Many people want God to forgive them even though they are unforgiving of others. That is not how it works. Jesus declares that the greatest commandment is to love the Lord with all your heart, soul, and mind. Notice that every moral principle you can think of falls under this commandment, including forgiveness. That first commandment covers it all! If we Love God with all our hearts, soul, and mind, we will Love and do right by others. Keep in mind that when we ask for forgiveness, we are to repent and not intentionally or willfully go back and do the exact same thing. We should never seek to live on grace. Yes, we all have sinned and have fallen short of the glory of God (Rom. 3:23, NKJV), but we are to strive for perfection as our Father in Heaven. So yes, ask for forgiveness, forgive others, but also, strive to sin no more. Read the scriptures below.

36 "Teacher, which is the great commandment in the law?"
37 Jesus said to him, "'You shall love the Lord your God with all your heart, with all your soul, and with all your mind.' 38 This is the first and great commandment.
—Matthew 22:36–38 (NKJV)

48 Therefore you shall be perfect, just as your Father in heaven is perfect.
—Matthew 5:48 (NKJV)

"Lead us not into temptation but deliver us from evil." This section implies and confirms the dynamics of the relationship between man and God. It confirms our place and God's place in our lives. He is the leader, the head, the load bearer. God said that He would not put more on us than we can handle. In context, He is talking about temptation. He said that He would always give us a way to escape. So this section is just tapping into that promise. We are seeking to be led by God and delivered. The term "deliver" in the dictionary means "to formally hand over (someone)." As for the word "origin," it means "away" and "set free" (*de-* is Latin for "away;" *-liver* derives from the Latin term *liberare*, meaning "to set free"). So this part of the sample prayer is requesting that God Himself formally set us free or set us away from ungodliness, as promised, which ties back into being in alignment with Him.

Activity #13a

1. Let's use Jesus's example to write out a prayer/petition. Complete the sections below *in your own words*. (I emphasize "in your own words" because this is you and your prayer to God, not anyone else. God accepts and Loves you as you are. So there is no need to try to use words and terms you never used to be someone that you are not. Keep this in mind throughout this activity.)

   _____

   _____

   _____

2. "Our Father in heaven." Remember that we first acknowledge those to whom we are petitioning. So in your own words, who are you talking to? Who is God to you?

   _____

   _____

   _____

3. Hallowed be your name." We know that we have the privilege to go in prayer and petition. When we pray, we are not talking to just anybody. This is God. We have discussed God's greatness earlier in the text. Recall from the text and utilize the Bible to express the unique and precious splendor of God in your own words. And let your chosen words further remind you just who you are petitioning.

   _____

   _____

   _____

4. "Your kingdom come, your will be done, on earth as it is in heaven." Remember, God gave us free will, but it is His desire that our will matches His Will, not the other way around. God put each of us here on earth for a purpose—His purpose. So our own agendas should

take a back seat to God's agenda for our lives. Plus, I can assure you that God's plan for our lives will turn out much better than our own! So in your own words, express that you want your will to align with God's Will. You want His plans to be done in your life and His Will to come into fruition.

_____

_____

_____

5. "Give us this day our daily bread." Express in your own words that God is your Source and that you need Him. This is where you cast your cares on Him. This is where you ask God for your heart's desires. Remember, the catch to this is that your heart's desires must align with His Will for your life. In addition, remember the word "our" is used in the example prayer, which means that you are to be considerate of others as you are going to God. We are to be blessings to others when He blesses us (overflow). Express your cares and petition below.

_____

_____

_____

6. "Forgive us for our trespasses as we forgive those who trespass against us." Keep Matthew 22:36–38, the greatest commandment, in mind when expressing in this section. We are to Love God with all our heart, soul, and mind. This covers all other commandments. Even though we are human, and we will make mistakes, we are to strive to be like God. Thankfully, when we do make a mistake or sin against God, He is merciful and forgives us. The caveat to that is that we must forgive each other. In this section, ask God for forgiveness for whatever you need forgiveness for. If you have trouble forgiving others, express that as well and ask God to touch your unforgiving heart. In addition, when you ask for forgiveness, remember the point is to strive not to commit the sin again. If you struggle with habitual sin, ask God to help you with this.

_____

_____

_____

7. "And lead us not into temptation, but deliver us from evil." While expressing in this section, remember that God must be the leader in your life. If we follow God, we cannot go wrong. When we are tempted to go outside of His Will, He will provide us a way to escape it. Also, God can set us free from any ungodliness. So whether it is doubts about the path

you have chosen, feeling lost, or you are struggling with habitual sin, express it here. Ask for guidance and deliverance.

_____

_____

_____

8. Close your prayer with thanksgiving, thanking God because whatever answer He gives and whatever He does will *always* be for your good! Then end the prayer with "in Jesus's Name" because Jesus said that God will do whatever we ask in Jesus's Name (that aligns with His Word).

⟶⟶◦⟵⟵

Whatever you ask in my name, this I will do, that the Father may be glorified in the Son.
—John 14:13 (ESV)

⟶⟶◦⟵⟵

Lastly, conclude the prayer with "Amen," an expression of agreement that derives from the Hebrew term *āmēn*, meaning "truth" or "so be it." Now express thanksgiving and confidence in God below. Don't forget to end in agreement with God (Amen).

_____

_____

_____

_____

_____

_____

_____

_____

_____

_____

_____

_____

_____

_____

_____

_____

Activity #13b

Now put it all together. Copy your prayer here. Then, read/pray it aloud.

_____

_____

_____

_____

_____

_____

_____

_____

_____

_____

_____

_____

_____

_____

_____

_____

_____

_____

_____

_____

_____

_____

_____

_____

_____

_____

_____

_____

_____

_____

_____

_____

_____

_____

_____

We have just broken down a prayer that Jesus gave to the disciples as an example. You used it to create your own prayer. This activity was just to acquaint you with praying. We have also covered in scripture the dos and don'ts of praying. Notice that it does not have to be elaborate. The Bible states that your words do not have to be many. "God, help me!" is a simple prayer, but it has power. Remember, God knows what you need and your heart's desires before you ever ask. He just needs your permission to manifest it on earth. So just talk to God as your Heavenly Father and remember who you are talking to when you go to Him. Pray. That is the bottom line.

Prayer is the component that connects us with God. God has equipped us with everything we need to fulfill the purpose He has given us. Here is an example to better illustrate this. Imagine a new vehicle with keyless entry. Now, imagine popping the hood and looking at its makeup. Take note of the complexities, the engine is attached to various hoses, wires, and other components such as the battery, radiator, the alternator toward the front of the engine, and the transmission underneath the engine. All these elements are needed for the vehicle to operate on the road. Okay, now imagine pushing the push-to-start button to start the vehicle but it does not start. What is the problem? I did say that this was a brand-new vehicle, and all components are intact. So why won't the vehicle start? It needs power. We did not mention the key, the source of power, in this illustration. Where is the key? Let's go and get the key and place it inside the vehicle. Now let's try starting it again. It starts! Power makes all the difference. Without the connection to that key, the vehicle is powerless despite the components it has within it because those components are intricately programmed to connect with that key. The vehicle can sit there, look pretty and impressive, and be admired on the showroom floor. However, if the vehicle is not within close proximity of the key, it will not have the power it needs to function.

Now let's go back and equate this to our prayer life. In the illustration, we are the vehicle, God is the key and source of power, and the proximity and connection is prayer. God has created us as "fully loaded" beings, but we must keep the connection through prayer with Him, our source of power.

If you need to hear it or see it, I will include it right now. *Prayer works.* No matter how simple or small or big the petition is, prayer works. However, let's delve into the constructs of more powerful prayers. I am going to list the constructs and explain each. Powerful prayers have the following:

✓ Does it align with God's Word, desires, and promises?
✓ Is the prayer bold or audacious?
✓ Is the prayer declarative?

Do you trust God and believe that He can and will fulfill the prayer?

"Does it align with God's Word, desires, and promises?," the first component, goes without saying but is one of the most important factors of prayer (Foster, *Praying Powerful Prayers*, 2019).

The things we ask of God must line up with God's Will for our lives. Bear with me on this ridiculous example, but let's go back to the example of my daughter asking her dad to take her and her cousin to the arcade. Do you think that her dad would have granted the request if it were to drive them around to shoot the neighborhood pets? That would not only be a "No," but it may also have landed her some clinical counseling sessions! This example is no more absurd than a woman praying that God grants the prayer that her illicit lover divorces his wife so that he can be joined in marriage to her, or vice versa. The practical example of my daughter hurting and killing animals is self-explanatory. The example about the individual praying for someone else to divorce is not only misaligned with the Word of God but is also an act of violence. Not only was divorce created by man (Moses) and was not God's idea, but it also forcefully rips apart the fabric of a vow made between the husband and the wife to God, which was to unite them to be one until they died. Surely, God does not mean for anyone to remain in a dangerous situation. I am not saying that divorce is an unforgivable sin. However, I am saying that God will not grant the petition that a person divorces his or her spouse to be joined with another person because there is nowhere in the Word of God that backs it. The important takeaway is that our petitions to God must be sanctioned within God's Word.

2 You want what you don't have, so you scheme and kill to get it. You are jealous of what others have, but you can't get it, so you fight and wage war to take it away from them. Yet you don't have what you want because you don't ask God for it. 3 And even when you ask, you don't get it because your motives are all wrong—you want only what will give you pleasure.
—James 4:2–3 (NLT)

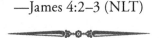

The next component, "Is the prayer bold or audacious?" is simple. God answers timid, limiting prayers. However, God also answers bold, audacious ones that have the power to part seas like He did for Moses in Exodus 14, topple walls of Jericho as He did for Joshua in Joshua 6, rain down fire and rain like He did for Elijah in 1 Kings 18, or bring a healthy child into the world to a young woman who was told she may not ever carry children and deliver that same woman from what was declared by doctors as her deathbed like He did for me!

God is for us! Let's not forget who He is. He is omnipotent! He is our Heavenly Father! So why pray rinky-dink, inferior, prayers? God desires for us to have an abundant life, lacking nothing. We are God's glory, His masterpieces to stand out for Him among those of the world as an example of His goodness. Why would He want us to be limited?! Think about this every time you go to Him in prayer.

The next element, "Is the prayer declarative?" has everything to do with confidence. To declare something is to make something known in a formal and explicit manner. Can you think of some things that people usually wait to declare until they are certain it will occur? People may wait to announce a pregnancy until the end of the first trimester. Remember when we discussed the probability of an embryo developing into a child to be born? (About 50/50.) The United States presidential election is another example. The *Chicago Daily Tribune* made the mistake of declaring, "Dewey Defeats Truman" on November 3, 1948, the day after incumbent United States president Harry S. Truman won an upset victory over New York governor Thomas E. Dewey in the 1948 presidential election. The newspaper was famously held up by President Truman at a public appearance as he smiled triumphantly at the error. This brings me to the hang-up and reason why most people that only pray timid prayers lack the confidence to pray bold prayers, fear of embarrassment. As you can imagine, the *Chicago Daily Tribune* must have suffered extreme embarrassment and damage to its reputation and credibility. That photo can still be googled and seen over seventy years later. The facts were incorrect for one of two reasons. It was either arrogance or the information was incorrect. Arrogance is different than confidence. Arrogance is the exaggeration of an individual's or a thing's ability or importance. If this were the case, the exaggeration would have been Dewey's ability to defeat Truman. Now if the information was incorrect, the problem lies in the source. What source did the newspaper rely on? Similarly, those who lack the confidence to pray bold prayers are uncertain about or have the incorrect source, which results in difficulty making declarative prayers because they fear falling on their face, frustration, and embarrassment if it does not come to pass. A declaration is a courageous act. This leads me to the next element, which coincides with declaring our prayers—trust.

Are we confident in our relationship with God and our proximity to Him? Are we certain of God's Word and His capabilities to do what we are asking? Ultimately, do we trust God and believe that He can and will fulfill the prayer? The difference between the confidence we have been discussing and arrogance is the choice of source. Who we gratify and acknowledge as our source depends on whether we are operating from a stance of confidence or arrogance.

If the source is anyone or anything but God, it is from a stance of arrogance.

Again, *rephrased*, and *elaborated*, an individual who believes in God is operating from a stance of arrogance if God (God's Word) is not the foundation and pillars in which the individual depends on.

One more time: Putting trust in your mom, dad, spouse, kids, friends, political figures, money, or anything else of or in this world, including yourself for your life indicates that you have made one or more of these limited factors your source, which means you are operating from a stance of arrogance because none of these are God.

I will prove why individuals that acknowledge God as their source operate from a stance of confidence with a rhetorical question. If arrogance is the exaggeration of abilities and importance, and God, our Heavenly Father and Creator, is the omnipresent, omniscient, omnipotent, sovereign

King of all kings, can His importance, His abilities, or anything about Him ever be exaggerated? Thus, confidence.

¹² Be happy because of the hope you have. Be patient when you have troubles. Pray all the time.
—Romans 12:12 (ERV)

¹⁹ This hope is a strong and trustworthy anchor for our souls. It leads us through the curtain into God's inner sanctuary.
—Hebrews 6:19 (NLT)

How do we acquire this confidence? Review that rhetorical question in the previous paragraph, particularly the portion pertaining to who God is. That information derives from God's Word. That's where the confidence comes from. We must know God's Word. It must be embedded in our hearts for us to trust in it. Otherwise, we can leave ourselves vulnerable, falling victim to arrogance by placing someone or something in God's position.

Our lives are determined by how we pray because God answers us on the level of our prayers. I have a few "poll questions" for you to answer. Answer truthfully.

- Do you believe that you must continuously speak during prayer?   YES   NO
- Is the prayer over once you have made your petition to God?   YES   NO

I will be honest. I used to think that the answers to both questions were "YES," but it is quite the contrary. Let's go back to the analogy of prayer being a petition as it is in the court system. What does the individual do after he or she makes the petition in a court setting? Is it over when the petition is made then? No, the petitioner must wait for the authority—in the court's case, the judge—to speak. The judge, or the authorizing official, may have a stipulation that needs to be achieved prior to granting the petition or important information pertinent to the petition. At that point, the petitioner is usually quiet because the lawyer, an individual that knows the laws and court's language, speaks to the judge on the petitioner's behalf. The lawyer speaks for and advises the petitioner on what to say and do in court. Also, the petitioner must wait for an answer.

So the answer to both questions above is "No." In the court example, we are the petitioner, God is the judge or authorizing official, the lawyer is the Holy Spirit, and the court is God's presence. When we pray, we speak, *and* we listen. Listening is the most important part. This is when we are quiet and allow the Holy Spirit to intercede and speak on our behalf. The Holy Spirit is always speaking to us. We must tune in by aligning with God, open and quiet our hearts, and pay attention to listen. Preacher Jeremy Foster mentions that we should be more into "listening prayers" instead of "list prayers." List prayers are OK, but pray listening prayers more often because we need to listen to what God wants us to say or what He wants to say to us. Prayer is a fellowship session between you and God; that connection is important to wholeness. Remember Jesus's example prayer, "Your kingdom come, Your Will be done on earth as it is in heaven." Also, remember that God is for us, His ways are always good, He always keeps His promises, and He is bigger than any problem any of us can ever face. So when you do speak, focus on praying God's promises instead of praying about your problem (Foster, *Praying Powerful Prayers*, 2019). Focus on the result that God has promised, not your current situation or trajectory in which your circumstance appears to be heading. We will have struggles and problems in life, but God has overcome them all, which means that we have nothing to worry about if we love the Lord and remain in His presence. Yes, we do speak in prayer, but let Him speak *for* you and *to* you as well.

SPIRITUAL FASTING

I'm about to get personal. At what lengths would you go to eat when you are hungry? Have you ever had cravings late at night? Did you make a run to a gas station or a fast-food place to satisfy that craving? How fast would you drive when you've realized that your favorite special or movie is not being recorded? Are you angry when you are unable to view the game live on television? How many times do you check your social media statuses for likes and comments after you have updated them? What lengths would you go to gain sexual satisfaction? Is sex or sexual gratification a necessity to function? Do you really need to stop every day after work to partake in happy hour? Did you really need that extra glass of wine? That cold one? That cocktail? All these questions are examples of how we satisfy our physical body, the flesh. When we purposefully abstain from doing things to feed the flesh, it weakens the power it has over our mind and soul, which allows the spirit to prevail. Thus, spiritual fasting.

So what is spiritual fasting? Spiritual fasting is the deliberate abstinence of physical gratification to achieve a spiritual goal (Evans, *The Importance of Fasting*, 2018). We are a spirit that has a soul, which lives inside of a dirt body (Munroe, *Spirit, Soul, and Body, Your Greatest Trouble*, 2018). Our bodies are also called flesh. Spiritual fasting is the denial of the flesh or anything that has to do with satisfying the body to gain a response from the spirit. It is a way of humbling yourself before God as it tells Him that you desire to please Him more than you desire to please your own body.

Recall the practical example of the key and the vehicle. The vehicle needs to be in close proximity to the key to obtain the power it needs to start. If you place the key inside the vehicle, it will start and function properly. Similarly, prayer connects us to God and gives us power. When we hide God's Word in our hearts, we will function properly. Let's kick this up a few notches. While prayer connects us to God for power like when the vehicle is connected to the key, spiritual fasting is like adding nitrous oxide (NOS) to the engine (Yes ... I am a *Fast & Furious* fan.). NOS significantly boosts the power of the engine. Spiritual fasting is the most powerful tool of prayer because when we combine the two, God can do immeasurable things *through*, *in*, and *for* us.

So how do you fast? What do you abstain from in a spiritual fast? How long do you fast?

How often do you fast? Well, an individual can fast on a variety of things. The most common thing to fast on is food, which is one of the easiest ways to satisfy the body. Over $1.77 trillion is spent on food every year in the United States alone (Martin, 2021)! You may even hear it in the medical field for blood work or certain procedures. The medical care provider may say something like, "Return to the facility fasting, nothing by mouth after midnight the night before." The difference between this type of fasting and spiritual fasting is the purpose. Spiritual fasting is not just abstaining from food or other pleasures but *replacing* those pleasures with God. It is a willing sacrifice that shows God that you know that you need Him more than food, social media, television, or whatever else consumes your heart and mind. Abstaining from food for anything other than replacing the act with God is just dieting. Abstaining from social media for a few days without replacing the time you would have spent on it with spending time with God is simply a break from social media. Again, an individual can fast on anything. The main component is what he or she *replaces* that thing with.

That time and energy must be replaced with connecting with God in addition to living aligned with God's Word.

Otherwise, it is *not* a fast. Review the scripture below.

—————◆—————

² For day after day they seek me out; they seem eager to know my ways,
as if they were a nation that does what is right and has not forsaken the commands
of its God. They ask me for just decisions and seem eager for God to come near
them. ³ 'Why have we fasted,' they say, 'and you have not seen it?
Why have we humbled ourselves, and you have not noticed?' "Yet on the day
of your fasting, you do as you please and exploit all your workers.
⁴ Your fasting ends in quarreling and strife, and in striking each other with wicked
fists. You cannot fast as you do today and expect your voice to be heard on high.
⁵ Is this the kind of fast I have chosen, only a day for people to humble themselves?
Is it only for bowing one's head like a reed and for lying in sackcloth and ashes?
Is that what you call a fast, a day acceptable to the Lord? ⁶ "Is not this the kind of fasting I have chosen:
to loose the chains of injustice and untie the cords of the yoke, to set the oppressed free and break every
yoke? ⁷ Is it not to share your food with the hungry and to provide the poor wanderer with shelter—
when you see the naked, to clothe them, and not to turn away from your own flesh
and blood? ⁸ Then your light will break forth like the dawn, and your healing will
quickly appear; then your righteousness will go before you, and the glory of the Lord
will be your rear guard. ⁹ Then you will call, and the Lord will answer;
you will cry for help, and he will say: Here am I. "If you do away with the yoke of oppression, with the
pointing finger and malicious talk, ¹⁰ and if you spend yourselves in behalf of the hungry and satisfy

the needs of the oppressed, then your light will rise in the darkness, and your night will become like the noonday. [11] The Lord will guide you always; he will satisfy your needs in a sun-scorched land and will strengthen your frame. You will be like a well-watered garden, like a spring whose waters never fail.
—Isaiah 58:2–11 (NIV)

Now let's discuss this scripture a few verses at a time. Remember, God is omnipresent, omniscient, omnipotent, and Loves us. I cannot stress that enough. Do not lose sight of that on this journey because it will serve as both a guide in keeping your paths straight and comfort during difficult times throughout your life. Verse 2 states that God's people *seem* eager to know His ways as if they were a righteous group of people that kept God's commands. They ask God for guidance in their lives and *seem* sincere about aligning with God. What does that tell us? God sees not only the action but also the heart or the intentions behind the action. Hence, omniscient. So when we do things to go through the motions or for an ulterior motive, God sees it because He knows our hearts. For example, when I was younger, I used to attempt "fasting" for three days. I remained out of alignment with God, I did not replace food with God or feed my spirit with His Word. Deep down, I wanted to lose a little weight and wanted to kickstart it with a "fast." It was quite difficult. So difficult that I never completed the full 3 days. Nothing changed in my life. There were no breakthroughs and the calamity I was experiencing continued because God remained on the backburner in my life. At the time, I didn't know what fasting really was and the power it holds. Years later, I learned the power of fasting and my relationship with God strengthened as I spent time with Him daily. Struggles came and I fasted for fourteen days. In the middle of the fast, everything I prayed about had been answered, and breakthroughs with my daughter and other circumstances occurred. This time, I found it difficult to break the fast! I was more productive; I had more peace than ever before; my heart was filled with joy and gratitude, which was prevalent and overflowed into everyone around me; and so much more! I give you these examples of life to say this. When you fast, be sure it is to seek a *spiritual goal*, not one of the flesh. When you do, get ready for our omnipotent God to open up the windows of heaven and rain favor and breakthroughs in your life that will overflow into others!

In verse 3, God's people ask Him *why* He had not seen or noticed them humbling themselves and fasting. Firstly, our omnipresent God is everywhere and sees *everything*. So the fact that the people are asking God this question reveals that they are disconnected from God. They do not know or have not taken the time to know who He is. That requires spending time with Him, which is what we do in a fast.

Secondly, their question was prideful. Is an individual that announces that they are humbling themselves really humble, or is it a show to gain credit for their actions? Think about that. Also, we are not to broadcast that we are on a fast for recognition. A fast is an intentional sacrifice of the heart and mind to glorify God. Instead, the people in this scripture glorified themselves. Later in verses 3 and 4, God explains that He did not acknowledge their fast because they were out of alignment with God. They pleased their flesh instead of Him by abusing or manipulating workers, displaying hostility, causing conflict with others, and fighting. God goes on to say, "You cannot fast as you do today and expect your voice to be heard on high." In other words, how can you expect me to honor your fast when you are so far from the Will of God?

Quick Survey Question:

What do you think would have happened if God had acknowledged the people's fast in the scripture? Do you think they would have become aligned with God anyway? Would they have just continued doing what they wanted to do? Would they have grown spiritually?

_____

_____

_____

_____

_____

_____

Well, in both examples, the instances about myself in my earlier years of "fasting" and the people in the scripture were similar. Our prideful hearts or intentions were not right. We were not aligned with God's Word, and we did not do it for a spiritual goal, which is why God did not acknowledge it. Review the scripture below.

16 "When you fast, do not look somber as the hypocrites do, for they disfigure their faces to show others they are fasting. Truly I tell you, they have received their reward in full. 17 But when you fast, put oil on your head and wash your face, 18 so that it will not be obvious to others that you are fasting, but only to your Father, who is unseen; and your Father, who sees what is done in secret, will reward you.
—Matthew 6:16–18 (NIV)

Going back to the scripture of Isaiah 58, in verse 5, God asks them the question that confirms that it is about the heart before the acts. He basically calls them out for doing all the perverse acts He mentioned and then performing rituals of humility as if it never happened. Please view the images below to gain a better understanding of what God is saying.

 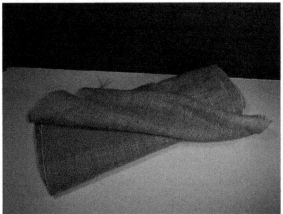

Remember, *we are a spirit* with a soul that is clothed in a body or flesh only to live here on earth. Our body is not the boss or the essence of who we are. So why do we go out of our way to please the body? A reed is a type of grass that blows or bows in whatever direction the wind blows. So it is not a coincidence that God made this analogy. The people in the scripture were led by the flesh (the body), which means they submitted, bowed, or gravitated toward whatever felt good to feed the flesh, which is the exact opposite of fasting, starving the flesh to strengthen the spirit. The expression "lying in sackcloth and ashes" is of Hebrew origin. Sackcloth is a coarse cloth (like a burlap sack) that was worn in a Hebrew custom when people dusted themselves with ashes, which symbolizes humility before God. Essentially, the people in the scripture attempted to clothe or cover themselves with this custom of humbleness with no intention of sincerely aligning their hearts with God. So God calls them out in this verse to let them know that He not only sees them, but He *sees* them. He sees them conducting this ritual that *they* call a fast, but He also sees their hearts, their intentions, their mindsets, and their perverse lifestyle. He basically says, "Is that what *you* call a fast?"

In verses 6 through 11, God tells us what He does through our spiritual fasting, that sacrifice and a dutiful heart are required, and transformation is guaranteed as He will respond on your behalf. In verse 6, God explains what *He* calls a fast, or what He chooses to acknowledge as a fast. God explains that the purpose of a fast is liberation, or to break free from something. Read verse 6 again. God speaks of loosening chains of injustice and not only untying the cords of the yoke to free the oppressed, but also breaking *every* yoke.

Keep in mind that a yoke is a wooden crosspiece that is fastened over the neck to attach to the plow cart, baskets, or other objects in which to pull, push, or to lift heavy loads. The term "yoke" derives from the Dutch term *juk*, which is originally from the Latin root word *jungere*, meaning "to join." Remember that we will have struggles, suffering, and burdens (John 16:33, NKJV), but we are comforted by the fact that God has already overcome the world and He promised never to leave or forsake us (Deut. 31:6, NKJV). So an individual that enters a fast the way that God intended will experience freedom from whatever spiritual hold in which he or she is suffering. Just because terrible situations or strongholds attach to your life, it does not mean that it is attached for good, because God is still God! For example, individuals can fast to break habits and addictions, overcome struggles in difficult circumstances, on behalf of other individuals, or be released of anything else that burdens them as long as it is a spiritual goal and in alignment with God. The results of a fast done God's way are freeing and life-changing.

Notice that verse 7 is a list of examples of how we should Love others in our daily lives. It is not so much about the list as it is about the posture of our heart. So not only must you relinquish something that gratifies you and replace it with God, but you also must strive to live a righteous life. Good character, a heart of gratitude, and service are practiced. It is not something that people are born with. Recall the section about our contaminated bloodline (with sin) and the example of a baby throwing a tantrum. This is why God sent Jesus—to save us from an eternity in hell, a place of pain and torture. So yes, we can choose to willingly practice these qualities as God gave us free will. When we do this and enter a spiritual fast, God transforms us. He renovates or rebuilds our life, and His power is endowed in us (v. 8). This verse also lets us know that when we go forth and lead with our righteousness or our right relationship with God, which produces peace and prosperity (Amplified Version), God's glory will be our rear guard, which confirms that we are covered! "Rear guard," or "rearguard," is a military term that refers to the soldiers positioned at the rear during a retreat of a body of troops to protect it against an attack. A retreat is a withdrawal from enemy forces. Remember, we are in spiritual warfare, fighting against authorities and rulers of darkness over this world and the evil spiritual forces in the heavenly realms (Eph. 6:12, NKJV). Think about it this way: When we choose to go forth in righteousness as our God has instructed, it simultaneously withdraws us from the enemy's forces as He (our omnipotent, omnipresent, omniscient God) covers us from behind and separates us from the enemy's influence. A good illustration of this is found in Exodus when God leads His people out of Egypt. God switched His positioning from the front of them to behind them, the most vulnerable place, which created a boundary between Egypt and Israel. Read the scripture below.

¹⁹ Then the angel of God, who had been traveling in front of Israel's army, withdrew and went behind them. The pillar of cloud also moved from in front and stood behind them, ²⁰ coming between the armies of Egypt and Israel. Throughout the night the cloud brought darkness to the one side and light to the other side; so neither went near the other all night long.
—Exodus 14:19–20 (NIV)

Notice how often God uses the word "then" after He explains spiritual fasting, beginning in verse 8. The term *then* means "after that," which confirms that something must occur before whatever is to come can occur. He concludes Isaiah 58:8–11 with, "If you will …, God will." He states that if we enter a spiritual fast as He has instructed it must be, then He will acknowledge it, answer us, and reveal Himself to us. If we retreat from wickedness or release ungodliness and embrace righteousness, His light will prevail in us and overtake the darkness, which will thwart the influences of our enemies. In addition, God guides and replenishes us as we need it, especially in our most troubling times (sun-scorched land in verse 11), when it seems that all resources have been depleted. Even then, God promises that despite our environment or what is happening around us or to us, He will provide in abundance. But first, we must make that decision—prayer, spiritual fasting, and a righteous lifestyle. Remember, God does not waver from His Word, as it is Law. If He said it, it is so because He has never gone back, nor will He ever go back, on His word.

"God is not a man, that He should lie, Nor a son of man, that He should repent.
Has He said, and will He not do? Or has He spoken, and will He not make it good?
—Numbers 23:19 (NKJV)

How long you fast can vary. You must go to God for what you should fast, how long you should fast, and how often you should fast. Collective events such as twenty-one days of prayer and fasting are common in churches, which aids in guiding and supporting individuals to stay on track in their fasting. However, it can be done collectively or by yourself. Also, an individual can fast for one day or forty days. Again, go to God for instruction; it is between you and God. Make sure that you are cleared by a medical professional when fasting from food for an extended period, especially if you're taking medication or have certain health issues. Again, there are other things that can be fasted.

Look It Up!

In case you are wondering, yes, it is possible! When I fast, I gain a deeper relationship with God, which radically transforms my life. I overcome situations and strongholds and accomplish so much. Here are a few other examples from the Word of God. Read it for yourself!

- Matthew 4:1–11 (NKJV)
  Jesus fasted for 40 days and nights in the wilderness, where the devil tried to tempt Him.

- Exodus 34:1–29 (NKJV)

  Moses fasted for forty days and nights when God spoke to Him on Mount Sinai and wrote the Ten Commandments.

- Esther 4–8 (NKJV)

  Queen Esther, her attendants, Mordecai, and the Jews in Susa fasted from food and water for three days before she (a woman) went to the king to submit a request, a crime punishable by death. Her request was not only honored, but an abundance of favor was given to her, Mordecai, and the Jews.

RELEASE THE WILDERNESS MENTALITY

Think back on who God is and who God says we are. We are loved and were purposefully created in God's image for His glory. So we must strive to have and uphold standards or a level of quality. No, we are not perfect. Even though we may make mistakes, stumble, or fail on this journey, we must actively seek God. Remember, God Loves and forgives. In this section, we will discuss some basic standards that will help you to carry and conduct yourself as a saved, free child of the Most High God.

In the movie *Harriet*, the story of Harriet Tubman, Harriet, a slave, ran away from the south to the north for her freedom. She made the decision to go all in on this journey through the wilderness all alone … or was she? Multiple sources stated that she had visions. She herself said that her visions were from God. The Holy Spirit guided her on every journey, especially on the journey to her own freedom. She had struggles along the way, but she persevered. When she made it to the north, she approached a man for directions. He gave her directions, and also told her that she had made it to the north. So she was free and needed to carry herself as such, not as a slave.

Harriet was born into slavery as Araminta "Minty" Ross. The slave mentality was all she knew. Then she traveled through the wilderness, on constant guard of slavers, wild animals, and other harmful elements. This wilderness mentality was a different type of survival. Nonetheless, she was still trapped, limited, and thus not yet free. When Minty made it to freedom, she chose to change her name to Harriet (her mother's name) Tubman (her husband's last name). In other words, she shed the name her oppressor gave to her and put on a new name. She was given a fresh start: food, clean clothes, a place to stay, and a job. After being enslaved for so long, she had to be taught how to carry herself. She consistently practiced this until it became a part of her. This resulted in her stepping into her purpose as an abolitionist, carrying out nineteen rescue missions and escorting over three hundred enslaved individuals to freedom.

Keep in mind, this five-foot-two woman traveled about ninety miles, mostly on foot, and crossed a river to be free. What do you think would have happened if she allowed fear to sink in and overtake her? Perhaps she would have just given up and gone back to the plantation. What would have happened if fear, tiredness, loneliness, frustration, or despair got the best of her? Maybe she would have surrendered her desire to be free. Then what? Well, she would not have fulfilled her purpose of freeing over three hundred slaves, while collaborating and changing the hearts of thousands along the way. Her legacy is celebrated because it transformed history. It makes me wonder how many events could have occurred to advance this world if the ones that God predestined to carry them out made it to spiritual freedom.

May I suggest to you that you are on your way to freedom! There will be rough terrain and darkness along the way in the wilderness, but when you get there, your victory will be that much sweeter! Let's go back to Harriet Tubman's story and apply it to the journey of spiritual freedom. Harriet decided to begin the journey to freedom just as you did when you accepted God's invitation and gave your life to Christ. Again, God will never leave you or forsake you (Deut. 31:8, NKJV). Just as He was with Harriet on her path through the wilderness, so He will be with you. An important takeaway from that is that you must be aligned with God to cross through the wilderness to freedom. What would have happened if Harriet decided to go left when God showed her that she should go right? We know that God would not have left her or let her go to the left alone because He does not break His promises. However, that decision might have prolonged her journey and made it more difficult. As you can imagine, Harriet must have developed a keener sense of survival and discipline in the wilderness. The word "wilderness" derives from the Old English term *wildērones*, which means "land inhabited only by wild animals." It is an inhospitable region or a position of disfavor. This implies that the wilderness is not a place meant for domesticated occupancy. It is a passageway, the gateway to freedom. The wilderness provided the setting to teach Harriet certain things. Perhaps you can say that it was her training day. We, as believers, have had or are going through our time in the wilderness. This can be viewed as the make-or-break season of an individual's life. It is like enlisting in the military and going through basic training or boot camp. Basic training is a stepping-off point to condition a soldier for their purpose, the mission that is to come. As you can recall in our previous discussion, we are in spiritual warfare with the devil. Going back to the story of Harriet Tubman, who did I say travel with her? It was just her and God. Sometimes isolation from others is necessary so that God can have your undivided attention. Harriet may not have made it to freedom if she had traveled with someone else on that first journey to the north. The wilderness conditions were so critical that there was little to no room for error. Another's negative opinions, doubt, or inaccurate advice could have been exponentially detrimental to her journey. Now the subsequent trips to lead others to freedom were totally different because her confidence in her relationship with God after that journey was solid and unwavering.

The most important part of her story is that she made it to the north and gained her freedom. She could have stayed in the wilderness, made her tent and clothes out of animal hide, fished, hunted, and picked berries for food, and lived a quiet, cautious, secluded life. But she did not do that. She went *through* the wilderness because she knew that her freedom, her purpose, and the things God set aside for her were on the other side. This is the biggest problem with young believers. ("Young" meaning new or spiritually immature Christians, not physical age) They fall victim to being content in the wilderness. Remember when I said that an individual can be saved but not set free? Remember when I admitted that I was saved at the age of seven but was not set free until thirty-seven? I pitched a tent in the wilderness for thirty years! I was content with just surviving off scraps and the bare minimum when He was trying to lead me to freedom. That is the absolute key purpose of this workbook. Although it is necessary as it is the gateway to freedom and purpose, I do not want anyone to be trapped in their wilderness.

Just as Harriet consistently practiced her authority and how to carry herself as a free woman, we must practice as well. God has saved you from sin. Yes. However, that does not mean that your mentality, habits, desires, and lifestyle has completely changed to align with God. It does not happen the moment you decide to give your life to Christ. It is a struggle within yourself to become aligned with the Will of God. Remember when we discussed how we do not have to teach a baby how to throw a tantrum or be selfish with a toy? That contamination will still wage war on us. We just need discipline to overcome it.

Let's go to the Word of God. In the Bible, water symbolizes chaos, death, or barriers. For Harriet Tubman, the Ohio River was the barrier on her journey to freedom. We will explore Numbers chapters 13 and 14. Here is some background to the story. Most of us have heard the story of how God used Moses to lead the Israelites out of slavery in Egypt in the book of Exodus. The word *Exodus* is a Greek term meaning "a mass departure of people." God used Moses to part the Red Sea so that the Israelites could safely cross on dry land to escape from the Egyptians. The Red Sea was the barrier between slavery and the wilderness. There have been multiple movies created about this story: *The Ten Commandments* (1923 and 1956), *Moses* (1995), the cartoon *Prince of Egypt* (1998), *Exodus: Gods and Kings* (2014), and *Patterns of Evidence: The Red Sea Miracle* (2020), to name a few. Well, Numbers chapters 13 and 14 is what happened after they crossed the Red Sea—the wilderness.

Activity #14

Turn to Numbers 13 and 14 in your Bible or on your Bible app and read both chapters in their entirety to gain a better grasp of this next section.

God used Moses to deliver them out of slavery in Egypt into a wilderness where He fed them with manna (bread) and quail. God promised to deliver them to a land flowing with milk and honey. When that time came, He led them to Canaan. The Israelites were to overtake the land as God had declared it. So Moses sent a representative of each of the twelve tribes of Israel to simply check it out and report back in forty days. When they returned, all except two of those representatives discouraged the rest of the Israelites from claiming their birthright. Those ten representatives saw that the land was indeed flowing with milk and honey, but they also noticed the size of the military and the stature of the men and panicked. So they spread discouragement by giving bad reports to the people. As a result, they stirred panic throughout their tribes, which led to people saying things like, "If only we had died in Egypt or in the wilderness" and "Wouldn't it be better for us to go back to Egypt?" Despite the miracles they had seen, the things God had already done, and where they had come from, they doubted and rebelled against God. So God forgave them, but he decreed that anyone (that was of age to vote) that rebelled against Him would not see the land He promised to their ancestors. Instead, He granted them the fates that they grumbled. They were to live and die in the wilderness. The land that they rejected was given to the offspring, the generation after them, but not before they endured the wilderness. They were to wander the wilderness for forty years, a year for each day they explored in Canaan until the last of that generation had died.

Caleb, who displayed an obedient heart, was the only one who wholeheartedly followed God by speaking out to carry out what God had instructed. Joshua agreed with him. God declared that both Caleb and Joshua would indeed see this land, and Caleb's descendants would inherit it. The crazy part is that after Moses told them what God had declared, they mourned. Then the next day, they set out to overtake the land of Canaan as God originally instructed! Notice that God did not give them a choice. He did not say, "Either go and claim the land of Canaan or wander in the wilderness for forty years until you die." Remember, God identifies Himself as a King, and a king's word is the law. God said what He said and meant it. Still, the Israelites decided that they were now ready to claim the land after God had determined their fate. It was as if they were saying, "Okay, God. You've twisted my arm. You've convinced me. We'll do it." (God is after our heart. He wants us to willfully follow Him.) They went to Canaan and met defeat.

Now let's break this story down to compare and apply it to our walk with Christ. God promised them that He would deliver them out of Egypt into a land flowing with milk and honey. First, He saved them from slavery in Egypt and brought them safely across a parted Red Sea. Notice that both the Israelites and Harriet crossed a body of water to obtain safety from oppression. Then He delivered them into the wilderness, an uninhabited space, a pass-through to the land He promised. God was there with them in the wilderness. He kept them safe and provided for them (provided quail and manna as food).

Do you see the similarities in what we have discussed in the story of Harriet Tubman and the Israelites? The only difference is that the Israelites did not follow God's instruction to go through the wilderness, which prolonged the fulfillment of His promise. Not only did they not obey Him, but they also treated Him with contempt, which is the opposite of glorifying. Can you recall the discussion about a king and his glory and how we are part of God's glory? God displayed so many miraculous works in their presence. Still, they doubted Him and talked (What comes out of the mouth defiles us [Matt. 15:18, NKJV]) themselves out of walking into God's promise. Then after God's decree, they decided that they were ready to do what God had originally said, but it was too late. It was not too late because God was not capable of doing what He promised. He knew that despite the exodus out of Egypt and the time in the wilderness, their hearts remained unchanged and out of alignment with His.

The takeaways from this are *obedience* and *alignment*. God's ways are not our ways. So things may seem unorthodox as it is occurring. Let's explore one more story about a wilderness transition. This is the story of how Jesus transitioned from His baptism to the wilderness. Read the scripture below.

> ⁹ *It came to pass in those days that Jesus came from Nazareth of Galilee, and was baptized by John in the Jordan.* ¹⁰ *And immediately, coming up from the water, He saw the heavens parting and the Spirit descending upon Him like a dove.* ¹¹ *Then a voice came from heaven, "You are My beloved Son, in whom I am well pleased."* ¹² *Immediately the Spirit drove Him into the wilderness.* ¹³ *And He was there in the wilderness forty days, tempted by Satan, and was with the wild beasts; and the angels ministered to Him.*
> —Mark 1:9–13 (NKJV)

Baptism is a celebrated and joyous occasion. It is a symbol of commitment to God. When an individual is baptized, he or she is usually fully submerged underwater for a moment. This represents death and resurrection through Christ Jesus. The death of the old occurs during the submersion, and the individual is made new when he or she arises from the water. It is a transition from old to new.

Notice that God acknowledged Jesus as His beloved Son, in whom He was well pleased, immediately after He came up from the water. This is before God died on the cross and rose from the dead. At this point in time, He had not yet carried out His purpose, but God is already pleased with Him. So it has nothing to do with His works. Jesus gave His life back to God and got baptized as a symbol of commitment to Him. Immediately following this, God accepted and acknowledged Him. This is also true for us. If you prayed that prayer earlier to accept God as your Savior, you were saved immediately. Even though you may not have yet fulfilled your purpose in God, He still calls you His beloved child, and He is already pleased with you. Now your training day has already begun.. Verse 12 states, "Immediately the Spirit drove Him [Jesus] into the wilderness." The Holy Spirit promptly steered Jesus into an uninhabitable place after a joyous occasion. This is the same Holy Spirit that had just descended from the parted heavens like a dove just before God confirms that Jesus is His beloved son with whom He is already pleased! Jesus had just experienced a perfect moment. I can imagine that Jesus gave off a sigh of satisfaction with a smile on His face, eyes still closed, and thought, *It doesn't get any better than this.* At least, that is what I would have done at that moment.

Then, all at once … wilderness. Have you ever had a time in your life where all was right with the world but then an event happened suddenly that turns your cloud 9 into calamity? Many people blame the devil for everything, even the slightest hint of opposition. Remember, in the previous examples, we discussed that the wilderness symbolizes boot camp or training, which is a form of conditioning resulting in transformation. It prepares us for our purpose, our blessings, and the next chapter of our life.

---

[11] For I know the plans I have for you," declares the Lord, "plans to prosper you and not to harm you, plans to give you hope and a future.
—Jeremiah 29:11 (NIV)

Sometimes it is not the enemy. It may be a training day in the wilderness to prepare you for something that you have prayed for or something that God is giving you in the future. Again, the plans that God has for us are always good, and we need to cleave to that when things get rocky. He is too good to just bless us with everything we ask for when we ask for it. We may not be ready for it. He saves us from ourselves.

Here is a simple example: Toddlers usually like colorful things. Imagine a toddler in pure bliss playing on the floor. As a parent, would you allow a two-year-old child to continue to play with marbles or small Legos? Hopefully, you would not, because the pieces would either go straight to his mouth or get thrown across the room. The child can see it, want it, and cry for it, but is not ready for that type of developmental toy. Instead, the child gets the plush basic development toy that sings and recites the alphabet, shapes, and colors. Reserve the marbles and Legos for later, when he or she is more mentally developed and able to play with them without getting hurt or hurting anyone.

Reflection

Reflect on your life. Can you recall some things that did not happen as planned but ended up working out for your good? Maybe it was the end of a toxic relationship, or a significant event postponed or canceled. Nevertheless, it somehow became a learning experience, and the results were better than you could have hoped. If you can think of such a story in your life, write a summary below. If you cannot think of anything, it is quite all right. Leave it blank and come back to it. It will happen soon enough!

_____

_____

_____

_____

Finally, in verse 13 of Mark 1:9–13, Jesus fasted for forty days and forty nights in the wilderness. This means that He sacrificed food to consecrate or devote himself to God for forty days and nights. So imagine how in tune Jesus was with God at this point! Afterward, Satan tried to tempt Jesus. However, Jesus overcame the wilderness and the temptation of the devil by exposing his lies and shunning him through scripture. Remember that fasting weakens the flesh while strengthening the spirit, which brings us closer to God. So the devil had little to no chance of infiltration! Again, it is imperative for us to know what God says. The Word of God is a weapon. It is the truth that extinguishes lies and annuls the deceit of the enemy. We covered this in activities #7a, #7b, and #7c when we learned to counteract the enemy's lies with scripture.

Now that you have given your life to Christ and relinquished your pain, struggles, and problems of your past to God, you have made it to the wilderness. This may not be what you want to hear, but the wilderness is what shapes us to be and to receive all that God has for us! Let me put it another way. We all go through wildernesses. Remember that we are a spirit (a part of God) with a dirt outer shell called a body. Earth is not the end game for us. There are two places our soul can end up when we depart from this earth—the kingdom of heaven or hell. Just as it is in the depiction of the story of Harriet Tubman, the people of Israel in the book of Exodus, and the story of Jesus's baptism and time in the wilderness, there is a pattern of water, then the wilderness. Pastor Robert Madu emphasized this in a sermon, stating that we were developed in our mother's womb, which was full of water (Madu, *Water and the Wilderness*, 2020). We are born into this world, but we will depart from it, which makes it a passageway. By this, we can conclude that we are born out of our mother's womb that is filled with water into the ultimate wilderness filled with patches of small wildernesses called earth.

Your new name has emerged: *Saved*. Your job, your purpose, was already predestined. You just allowed God to clear the path to your purpose by removing the baggage you have been carrying. The things that once paralyzed you will fade away in the wilderness as you develop and grow closer to who God has called you to be. So take heart and press on *through*! Your next stop is spiritual freedom, where you will live out the purpose God has prepared just for you. On this journey, you must be mindful of where you dwell, what you put on, how you carry yourself, and the company you keep.

An Important Tip for Releasing the Wilderness Mentality

We must stay close to God and continually seek to do His Word even when we stumble or make a mistake. It will happen, and He knows it. He is omniscient, remember? So it is not a surprise. Also, remember that He is our Heavenly Father, who Loves us unconditionally and is already pleased with us. So stay close.

People tend to shamefully shy away from God when they stumble. Have you ever noticed how toddlers or young kids get really quiet when they are in another room doing something that they have no business doing? For example, you have given them specific instructions and rules about scissors. Still, the child decides to give himself a haircut, cut the bedsheets, and oddly enough, trim the custom shower curtain in the guest bathroom. You never hear a peep out of him. In fact, you cannot find him. He has hidden himself, just like how Adam and Eve hid after they first disobeyed God's instructions about the tree (Gen. 3:8–10, NKJV). This tends to be what we do when we know we have sinned. When we stumble, we let that guilt keep us from God, which leaves us vulnerable.

Eventually, we allow the shame of that sin to keep us away from God for so long that we become comfortable living in sin. An example of this would be a toddler beginning the potty-training process. Toddlers will comfortably run around playing in a dirty diaper for as long as you let them. The toddler has been trained and knows how to ask for the potty but decides against it to carry on with what he is doing. When he soils himself, he tends to find the farthest corner to play in so that he is free to continue playing. At this point, he may not even respond when he is called. He is too busy living his life! Little does he know that keeping on a dirty diaper for a long period of time is harmful, causing skin rashes, the spread of bacteria. and toxicity, which leads to infection and sickness. In the same way, when we sin and shy away in shame, God continues to call for us to draw us near Him. He knows where the path that you are on will lead you. So make a conscious effort to stay close to Him no matter what.

⁵ This is the message we have heard from him and declare to you: God is light; in him there is no darkness at all. ⁶ If we claim to have fellowship with him and yet walk in the darkness, we lie and do not live out the truth. ⁷ But if we walk in the light, as he is in the light, we have fellowship with one another, and the blood of Jesus, his Son, purifies us from all sin. ⁸ If we claim to be without sin, we deceive ourselves and the truth is not in us. ⁹ If we confess our sins, he is faithful and just and will forgive us our sins and purify us from all unrighteousness. ¹⁰ If we claim we have not sinned, we make him out to be a liar and his word is not in us.
—1 John 1:5–10 (ESV)

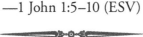

THE WILDERNESS PROCESS: SPIRITUAL WARFARE

Has your mind ever wandered off to other things while you were driving on a long, straight road? How about your commute from work to home? Have you ever slipped into autopilot? After a while, you are home, or almost at your destination, but you do not recall the drive. Perhaps it is just me. There have been multiple times where I have planned to stop at the grocery store after work but found myself on my street headed home. I did not forget. It was in my mind to do, but my mind's autopilot and muscle memory took over when I began listing things I needed to do once I got home.

Let's talk about lifestyle, the ultimate autopilot. We know, want, and try to do better; but it either gets too difficult to attain or slips through the cracks of higher priorities. How about making a New Year's resolution? Did you start off well but gradually reverted to old habits? Did you use logic to justify the need for procrastination?

Here are some examples:

I need to make healthy dieting choices, but it is wasteful to throw food away, even if it is unhealthy.
I know that I need to end this toxic relationship, but we have known each other for fifteen years.
These habits are not in alignment with God's Will for my life, but I picked it up at a young age and it is second nature.
I need to read my Bible every day and pray at least an hour a day to have a closer relationship with God, but there is no time because I am a single parent and work twelve-hour shifts.

Again, maybe it is just me.

Reflection

Read the scripture written by Apostle Paul below. Can you relate to what he is saying?

¹⁴ We know that the law is spiritual; but I am unspiritual, sold as a slave to sin. ¹⁵ I do not understand what I do. For what I want to do I do not do, but what I hate I do. ¹⁶ And if I do what I do not want to do, I agree that the law is good. ¹⁷ As it is, it is no longer I myself who do it, but it is sin living in me. ¹⁸ For I know that good itself does not dwell in me, that is, in my sinful nature. For I have the desire to do what is good, but I cannot carry it out. ¹⁹ For I do not do the good I want to do, but the evil I do not want to do—this I keep on doing. ²⁰ Now if I do what I do not want to do, it is no longer I who do it, but it is sin living in me that does it.

²¹ So I find this law at work: Although I want to do good, evil is right there with me. ²² For in my inner being I delight in God's law; ²³ but I see another law at work in me, waging war against the law of my mind and making me a prisoner of the law of sin at work within me. ²⁴ What a wretched man I am! Who will rescue me from this body that is subject to death? ²⁵ Thanks be to God, who delivers me through Jesus Christ our Lord! So then, I myself in my mind am a slave to God's law, but in my sinful nature a slave to the law of sin.

—Romans 7:14–25 (NIV)

The mind is like a computer. It requires energy to process things as it downloads all that we experience with our five senses. Our minds seek to conserve our energy by developing a system through conscious and subconscious processing. The subconscious part of the mind automates much of what we do. Examples of these are basic life functioning, learned behavior, habits, and fight-or-flight responses. Like a computer or a cell phone's autocorrect or autofill feature, the brain downloads these actions, and they are imprinted to conserve our energy. This way, the behaviors become second nature. We do not have to think about them to do them. The subconscious part of the brain also forms our memories based on our knowledge and experiences, which develop our attitudes. Ninety-five percent of our behaviors and reactions happen at the subconscious level (Sentis, 2012). So you can see how influential the subconscious part of the mind is. The conscious, however, is the discipline portion of the brain, as it is responsible for higher-level thinking. Even though the subconscious influences nearly everything we do, the conscious portion of the mind can reprogram that subconscious portion, which transforms our habits, attitudes, reactions, and behavior.

The subconscious portion of the mind is our heart, and it acts as a hard drive. It stores memories, repetitive actions, and experiences for processing and future usage. Therefore, our thoughts dictate our actions. Our repetitive actions become habits and habits become a lifestyle. It all starts with our minds. It is quite difficult to change our mindsets. The Bible states that as a man thinks in his heart, so is he (Prov. 23:7, NKJV). What we think is in our hearts. Whoever's information and influences are more prominent will win that tug-o'-war battle for the soul. Therefore, boundaries are a must. Whoever or whatever controls our heart controls our life. Our heart is our soul, which is made up of our will, mind, and emotions (Munroe, *Control Your Mind*, 2019). Dr. Myles Munroe states that an individual can be saved and believe in God but still be in bondage mentally. This means that an individual can physically be in church, but in an agonizing prison within his or her mind. As long as souls remain lost and individuals are misaligned with God, the enemy does not mind church attendance. Physical attendance is easy. That is just showing up. Becoming saved by accepting God as your Lord and Savior happens in seconds. The conversion of the soul is much more complicated. God gave us free will, which means we have the freedom to program our minds with whatever content we desire, even if it does not align with His Will. God wants our will to align with His, but He does not force it. We have a choice. Remember, we are in spiritual warfare. The war is a battle for our souls. The devil, the enemy, is after our soul as well, which is why it is so important that our minds are reconditioned to align with God's Will.

12 Therefore, I urge you, brothers and sisters, in view of God's mercy, to offer your bodies as a living sacrifice, holy and pleasing to God—this is your true and proper worship. ² Do not conform to the pattern of this world, but be transformed by the renewing of your mind. Then you will be able to test and approve what God's will is—his good, pleasing and perfect will.
—Romans 12:1–2 (NIV)

Notice that the above scripture says to be transformed by the renewing of your *mind* because your mind is where transformation begins. It is where your breakthrough is first manifested. Your mind is where all actions begin, which is why there is a constant war going on between the flesh and the spirit for control over it. Review the illustration below.

THE ULTIMATE TUG-A-WAR

The Spirit and the flesh are at battle to win over the soul.

Illustration Depicts Dr. Munroe's Sermon: "Control Your Mind"

Let's discuss an example that will better explain the above illustration. Bob has been married for seven years and has three small children. He and his wife rarely have quality time for intimacy and have frequent arguments. Bob has been newly partnered with a single, attractive female colleague that recently transferred. As time passes, they become comfortable with each other. They gradually begin giving each other compliments, making flirtatious comments, and giving suggestive body language. What is happening? The flesh, the body, has collected data from the five senses and transmitted it to the brain, which conveys it to the heart/soul. Bob's flesh has gathered that his colleague is visually attractive, smells good, and sounds good. On occasion, he and his colleague trade touch through playful hitting and accidental body brushing. The body registers that it feels good as well. At the same time, the spirit declares whether this experience and behavior are in alignment with God's Will. In this case, it does not align with God's Will because Bob is married and is lusting after another woman. This information is transmitted to the heart/soul as well. Now Bob's soul has to decide on what action to take. Does Bob yield to his body and continue this illicit relationship with his colleague to satisfy the flesh? Or does Bob end the inappropriate relationship with his colleague, maintain professionalism, and make time to reconcile and bond with his wife? Flesh or spirit? This is the ultimate tug-o'-war.

Life is simple. We've all heard the saying, "You are what you eat." Individuals with a consistently healthier diet tend to be healthier than individuals with a consistently unhealthy diet. This is also true with our minds and heart. We are what we consume. That is, we are the things we allow to consistently enter our minds. This includes what we hear, see, and expose ourselves to. Whoever or whatever controls your heart controls your life. The information that you expose yourself to the most will become influencers. Those more prominent influencers will win that tug-o'-war battle for your soul. This is why it is important to fill ourselves with godly influencers and create and enforce boundaries to limit ungodly or evil things in our lives. Evil or ungodly things are all around us and are impossible to completely get away from, but don't give yourself up willingly.

The Wilderness Process: Patterns of the Wilderness

We will be tested throughout life, just as Jesus was in the wilderness. So we must know God and His Word and know ourselves to block ungodly influences. We will spend our lives going in and out of wildernesses, in and out of training. Do we not undergo training when we acquire promotions at work? How about a better career opportunity? Are orientation and on-the-job training not required? Expansion requires preparation, hence the wilderness. If we desire for our territory to be expanded, we must be prepared for all that it encompasses. Just as Jesus was tempted and tested in the wilderness, we will also be tested. I will give you an example from my life. When I was younger, I asked God for a more prestigious career. At that time, the prayer I prayed was because I was uncomfortable with who I was. I had low self-esteem and tried defining myself with earthly titles and statuses because I placed my value in labels that were created by other human beings that had no hand in creating me. I aspired to be a special agent or a detective, or some other impressive title with the FBI, CIA, or any of the other government agencies because I thought it would add value to my life. Once I prayed that prayer, it seemed that everything fell apart at my job, in my marriage, and with my daughter. Conflicts escalated at work, my husband and I were estranged, and my daughter's social development was lacking. At the time, we did not know she had autism. She struggled in school and could not comprehend and hold a simple, independent conversation. I failed spiritual tests over and over as I went deeper into my wilderness. It became a cycle that worsened with each rotation until it finally broke me. I thought it was finally going to happen for me when I made it to the final stages of the hiring process for quite a few prestigious agencies, but the hiring process for these positions was canceled. After that, I was angry with God. I lamented to Him, asking why He has not delivered me out of this whirlwind of a life. My motivation and drive were completely shattered. Still, I never stopped talking to God. In public, I displayed a façade, at home, a pity party within myself. Soon my health began to fail due to prolonged periods of stress. A light switched on when one of my friends told me that she looks up to the godly woman, wife, and mother that I am and strive to be better because of it. I was not the person she exaggerated me to be, but I wanted to live up to it. So I began to align myself with God. Slowly, things began to ease. When my posture changed, my circumstances changed. I assumed a more active role at work by motivating employees, I drafted lesson plans and performance goals for my daughter, and I prayed for my husband more than I prayed for myself. Eventually, God removed the individuals that were seeking to harm me, and there was progress at home. Looking at that situation now, I see that God was preparing me for something greater all along. I did not obtain the glorified government agency title I initially prayed for—I received much more. In that wilderness, I learned how to posture myself, how to motivate and influence, how to support my daughter's development, and how to trust in God. That wilderness led me to a new passion and discovery of the gift of motivating and improving organizational structure for productivity. It led to my pursuit of a graduate degree in I/O psychology. It also resulted in me ending toxic relationships and gave me the ability to filter toxic comments from individuals who are close to me. This book is the product of growing through that wilderness. I learned to love and help others right where they are without allowing it to negatively impact me. I say all of this to make this point. I would not have been prepared for all that God has me doing now if I had not grown through that wilderness. I asked Him for expansion, and He put me in training to receive it. Review the graph below to grasp the pattern of transformation, growth, and blessings.

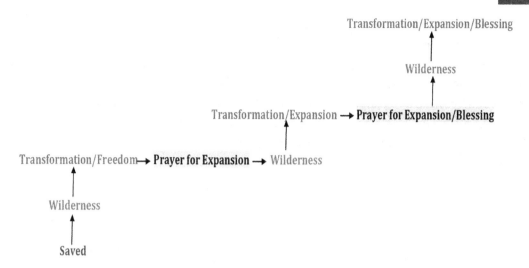

Notice that the diagram mimics progressive steps of elevation and expansion. Let's follow the graph as we discuss a scenario. Claire accepts God as her Lord and Savior. She is now *saved*. She has a bit of a hard time converting her lifestyle to align with God's Will for her life. Her peers attempt to pressure her to do and say things that she used to do and say. Her significant other of four years moved out, and some of her friends faded out of the picture. She is tempted to go places she used to go. She seems to be *tested* at every turn in this wilderness. Nevertheless, it gets easier for her, and she begins socializing with other saved individuals. They share their experiences, support each other, and *transform* together. Claire prays for a husband that is a man of God. Her ex-boyfriend returns to reconcile. They try for a while to make things work, but Claire's new lifestyle of sexual abstinence until marriage, Bible studies, and mission group meetings grow unappealing to him. Although she passed the test and weathered that wilderness, she was still deeply saddened and brokenhearted from the breakup. Yet she lamented and stayed in alignment with God. Claire continued her journey and kept the faith. A year later, she meets a man in the mission group that she enjoys spending time with. He is a man of God and has the same beliefs and values as Claire. Three years later, her prayer was answered. They are married and have a fulfilling marriage. Claire and her husband have demanding jobs, but they want to start a family. Claire desires to fully devote her time to being a mother and wife but cannot financially afford to resign and start a family. They pray that God would bless them with children and give them the financial means to care for them. Two years later, Claire becomes pregnant with twins, but their financial circumstances have not changed. Even though the family struggles financially, they stay aligned with God and trust in Him. Family and friends help care for the twins when Claire returns to work. Three years later, Claire's husband assists a man at a gas station with a flat tire. He ministers to the man and exchanges phone numbers. The man hands Claire's husband his business card. He is the CEO of the company he has just interviewed for. After reviewing his credentials, the man offers Claire's husband a higher position, so he is making over twice the salary. With twin toddlers and one on the way, Claire is able to resign and stay at home full-time to care for her family.

Did you notice that the process was not immediate? It may take days, weeks, months, or years for our prayers to come to fruition. It happens when God declares that it is supposed to happen, not when we think we need it to happen. We have a perfect twenty-twenty vision only in hindsight. We do not know the future. So we do not know what we will or will not be ready to handle. However, God is omniscient and places the answer to our prayers precisely where they need to be.

PRINCIPLES FOR THE WILDERNESS: BOUNDARIES AND STANDARDS

I will begin by asking a few questions. Answer the following questions below based on what we have discussed and your understanding. We will discuss this in this section.

Activity #15

1. Does who we are dictate the lives we lead? _____
   a. Should it? Why or why not? _____
   _____
   _____
   _____

2. Why do you think it is important to know where you are spiritually and mentally?
   _____
   _____
   _____

3. Why is it important for us to study and know the Word of God?
   _____
   _____
   _____

Imagine that you are carrying items on your back in a backpack and in both hands from one side of a massive room to the other. There are crates, boxes, glass objects, and spills on the floor, low-hanging objects swinging from the ceiling, and various noises from equipment throughout the area. Sounds like madness, doesn't it? As you begin to maneuver your way to the other side, all the lights are shut off. It is pitch-black. Even if you were able to hold your hand out in front of your face, you would not see it. Rhetorical question: would it be easier to move within this space with or without light?

Let's try one more image. Imagine that you work for an advertising company. Your supervisor gives you the task of creating an advertisement for an automotive company. The only aspects you know about the company are the name and that it deals with automobiles in some fashion. You do not know the mission or purpose of the company. Is it a car dealership that sells cars or trucks? If so, what kind? Does it sell auto parts? Does it conduct automotive repairs? Rhetorical question: do you need to know the purpose and type of the company to create and effectively complete your assignment?

These are some far-fetched examples, but there is a point. Knowing makes all the difference in the process of progression and victory. Knowing your identity and where you are spiritually are key components of setting standards in the wilderness. The wilderness is designed to test us at every turn, which is why it is imperative to solidify these components. What happens if you carry on through life without checking your alignment with God? Well, God's Word is a lamp unto our feet and a light unto our path (Ps. 119:105, NKJV). So chances are, you would walk around in spiritual darkness, just as I depicted in that dark space, which will heighten the probability of stumbling and going off course. In the movie, *Harriet*, Harriet Tubman pauses at the forks in the paths to discern God's voice and vision for her path. She checked her alignment and knew where she was because God was her compass.

Knowing our identity does and should in fact dictate our lives because our identities should directly correlate with our standards. The word "standard" derives from the word "stand," which means maintaining an upright position, supported by one's feet. Have you ever heard the expressions "What do you stand for," "I will not stand for that," or "Stand up for what you believe in"? What does this all tell us? Be it low or high, our standards are embedded deep in us, and it directly correlates with the core of our identity, or what we believe our identity is.

This brings me to the two principles that dictate every facet of our lives, especially our time in the wilderness. Solidifying these principles as your foundation should align the subsequent principles. We have discussed them both but will build on it in this section. The first key principle is to know and remember who God is. The second key principle is to know and remember who you are. All other principles, including the second principle, either spawn from or tie into that first principle. God is our creator and Heavenly Father. So knowing Him is knowing ourselves.

Activity #16/Review

Do you remember who God is? Go back and review the section that defines who He is. We will revert to that section numerous times in this section. So let's do another breakdown to review who God is below for your recollection.

- God is Love. What is Love? Kind,_Patient, _____
  _____
  _____
  _____

  o What does perfect Love drive out? _____
- God is King of kings. What are the three qualities of a king?
  _____
  _____
  _____

- God is omnipresent, omniscient, and omnipotent. Define each term.
  Omnipresent – _____
  Omniscient – _____
  Omnipotent – _____

Now review your submission once more. Love. All-powerful. All-knowing. All-present. King *over all* kings. This is our Creator, the One who calls us His children and heirs to His kingdom! How does that make you feel? Does it ignite something inside of you? Does it give you the confidence to hold your head up and walk a little straighter? It definitely does that for me!

Activity #17

Now let's review who you are. Refer to the Word of God and review the section that defines who you are as needed to answer the following question.

- Who are you?
  _____
  _____
  _____

Recall the discussion of who we are. We are not defined by what we do, where we come from, or any attributes we may have. Again, we are a spirit (God's Spirit) inside of an earthly or dirt body. What does this tell us? Well, can a fish survive out of water? No. It needs to be in the water just as we need to be in Christ. We need a connection with God because the very core of our being is of Him. He is our source. We need that connection to live out the unique purpose that God has for us. If we know that, then everything else falls into place. Knowing who we are clearly defines our principles, proclamations, and standards. Here is an example.

Because of who I am,

- I need to stay close to God.
- I need to study His Word, fast, and pray to Him on a regular basis to discern His voice.
- I need to set standards and boundaries that align with God's Will for my life.
- I have a purpose.
- No weapon formed against me shall prosper because He has overcome the world, healed me by His stripes, and covered me with His blood.
- I have dominion over the earth, and I am an heir.
- I can do all things through Christ who strengthens me.

Activity #18

Now that you know who you are, make a list (just as in the previous example) of principles, proclamations, and standards that have been made clear for you. Make your list specific to your life and situation. List at least five in the section below.

Because of who I am:

1. _____
   _____

2. _____
   _____

3. _____
   _____

4. _____
   _____

5. _____
   _____

6. _____
   _____

7. _____
   _____

Knowing who God is tells us who we are in God. And knowing who we are in God simplifies our lives. The boundaries and standards required to live an aligned life with God become clear.

What type of things might you encounter in an actual wilderness? There may be wild animals, deadly insects, poisonous plants, lots of trees that obstruct your vision, and vines to stumble over. Yes, there may be fruit and other edible things, but which are safe to consume? Yes, there may be streams of water, but will all sources of water be safe for consumption? How does an individual sustain, thrive, and maintain preservation while enduring the wilderness? Surely, there must be boundaries and standards put in place. In the same way, life on earth, the wilderness, has not been child-proofed for us. There are no bumpers or cushions that prevent harm, guard rails or safety gates to keep us on track, or safety locks to keep us away from things and places we should not go, which is why we need boundaries. In this section, we will discuss boundaries, their importance, and how to set and consistently keep them.

This leads us to our first subcomponent, setting boundaries and standards. A boundary is a choice that creates a rule or standard. Life is comprised of a series of choices. Our choice is our power. It is the will that God has blessed us with. Our will or the power to choose is the most powerful yet most dangerous component we possess. It gives us the power to make choices and create standards that shape our life, which can either align or go against God. Some people are terrified to make a decision, create boundaries, or set standards out of fear of its consequences. However, it becomes easier when we realize that the questions have already been answered, the boundaries have been set, and standards have been put in place. The answers have been written for us in our manual, the Word of God. Because of who we are in God, our boundaries and standards have been predetermined. Remember, God's ways are always good. So His boundaries for our lives are *always* good. It is our choice whether we adhere to or go against His Word.

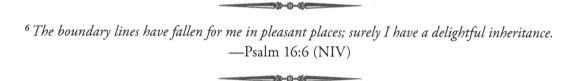

⁶ The boundary lines have fallen for me in pleasant places; surely I have a delightful inheritance.
—Psalm 16:6 (NIV)

Boundaries preserve freedom. It is not a leash or bondage chains but a fence. A fence serves as a boundary and protection for freedom, while a leash restrains and limits. Here are some examples. My brother's dog, Kurama, saw a fence as a restraint and wanted to be free. So he would climb over the fence and roam the neighborhood. After a few of those Houdini stunts, he got hit by a car and had to be rushed to the vet to treat his injuries. Kurama had no idea that the fence, that boundary, was for his protection. When I was younger, my brother and I had a German shepherd named Missy. The next-door neighbor had three pit bulls. A hurricane blew part of our fence down. So we put Missy on a leash outside until the fence was repaired. The next-door neighbor's dogs would come into our yard and attempt to eat Missy's food. They succeeded a few times. When the fence was repaired, the pit bulls dug under the fence to invade our backyard, only to find that Missy was no longer on a leash. Two pit bulls were severely injured, the other went back to its yard. What could happen if a high-rise hotel balcony had no railings? What is the purpose of a toilet stall in a public restroom? Is it not for privacy to protect the individual's freedom to freely use the toilet? Again, boundaries are protection, not restraints.

Before we go any further, let's pause and discuss self-love. This term is used quite often in our society. You hear and see it everywhere: "more self-love," "love yourself," "#selflove." What does it really mean? More importantly, what *should* it mean? Well, we know that God said to love our neighbor as we love ourselves. What did God mean by this? This goes back to the beginning of this text when we discussed the definition of Love. Do you remember what love is? Let's recap. Love is an action and not a condition-driven emotion. God commands it, and it is God. Hmm … When God said to love our neighbor as we love ourselves, it did not mean to obsess over our neighbor, put our neighbor first every time, or work hard to please my neighbor. Guess what. If that isn't how you love your neighbor, it can't be how you are supposed to love yourself! None of the things previously mentioned reflect true self-love. Self-Love is focusing on God who *is* Love. Chan (2021) said it best when he stated that giving yourself to God is the ultimate Self-Love. It is okay to treat yourself. Just don't let any of the things you do to please yourself (or others for that matter) come before God.

If we replace "love" in the term "self-love" or "love yourself" we would get the following:

- *Yourself* is to do an action that *isn't* driven by emotion or conditions.
- *Yourself* is *commanded* by God.
- *Yourself* is to be *close* to God.

Let's go in-depth about the importance of relational boundaries. In this context, a boundary can be defined as a threshold that creates a standard or space between the individual and the other person. In other words, it is a line that is drawn that depicts a point in which either the individual or others are not to cross. Yes, this will be allowed. Or no, this will not be allowed. Yes, I will do this. Or no, I will not do this. An example of a physical relational boundary would be personal space. Would you allow strangers to walk up and palm your face? Yes, or no? Now we have a much larger problem on our hands if you would be comfortable allowing this. However, most people would not allow this, nor would they walk up and palm a stranger's face. It is a choice. Review the chart below.

TYPES OF BOUNDARIES

Physical boundaries – Refer to the body, privacy, and personal space

Examples: A person palming your face; Public Displays of Affection

Intellectual boundaries – Involve ideas and beliefs

*Examples: Showing respect for different views and ideas (Note: Not everyone will think like you, but you must love
everyone and categorize accordingly to properly set your boundary.*

Time Boundaries – Cover all the chronological factors for an individual's presence, attention, and energy.

Examples: One-on-One; Quality Time; Undivided attention

Material Boundaries – Refer to respect for one's own and/or individual's belongings

Examples: Timely returning other people's property intact after borrowing; Theft or destruction of property (violation); Allowing others to use or borrow money or possessions as a means of control (violation)

Emotional boundaries - Involve separating your feelings from another's feelings. (Remember, emotions have no place in setting and upholding boundaries)

Examples: (The following violate emotional boundaries.) Taking responsibility for another's feelings, letting another's feelings dictate one's own, sacrificing one's own needs to please another, blaming others for one's problems, and accepting responsibility for theirs.

(Selva, 2020)

At times, boundaries may be difficult to enforce, but the benefits significantly outweigh this drawback. Healthy boundaries help enforce our identities, and promote good emotional, mental, and physical health while influencing others by developing autonomy (Selva, 2020). So boundaries and standards are healthy when set correctly and consistently implemented. Boundaries should be set and implemented in every relationship and every aspect of your life. These aspects include mental, physical, emotional, and spiritual. An example of a boundary and standard that covers all four is abstinence from sexual activity before marriage. In this case, the boundary involves all four aspects: The body (the physical act), the psychological or mental attachment that creates soul ties and emotional strain, and the original purpose and design of sex by God (spirituality).

We form relationships within these four aspects, which must be protected and maintained. Imagine a nice, cozy, cottage-style home. The yard is exquisitely manicured with a beautiful fountain and flower garden as its focal point. Now take that same cottage-style home and fast-forward five years in time without protection and maintenance. How does it look? Is it still nice with a beautiful focal point? No. The overgrown grass, shrubs, and trees cover the dead weeds–infested garden and fungus-filled fountain. Mildew and dirt now hide the original color of the house. The shutters have been forced off by the out-of-control bushes that lined the home and siding, and shingles have been scraped off by the branches of the trees, which causes water leaks and mildew inside the home. Rodents and other creatures lurk among the thick dead grass and often make their way into the home through siding gaps. Can you see it? So without monitoring and maintenance, the home is falling apart and wasting away.

What about us? The Word of God states that God dwells or lives in us. We are a resident, a home for God, and it is our responsibility to monitor and conduct maintenance. In that cottage-style home example, did you notice that everything that destroyed the home was either natural or supposed to be there? The home was not destroyed by an outside factor such as looters. Grass, trees, plants, bushes, and animals in their natural element were the alleged culprit. But let's take a closer look at this allegation. Did God give dominion to any of the influences previously listed? Or did God breathe His Spirit into and give authority over the earth to mankind? Was our body not created from the earth? Did God give us free will? What does this all mean? The owner of that cottage-style home has dominion over it just as we have dominion over the earth. Specifically, we have dominion and free will over our body or temple, and it is our responsibility to monitor and maintain it so that it remains a suitable dwelling place for God, just as the owner of the cottage-style home should have done in the example. Standards derive from boundaries to serve as maintenance for the soul (Foster, *Balanced Boundaries*, 2020). A boundary preserves your heart, in which all things flow. In the visual of the cottage-style home, the owner should have set a boundary for the home and property. For example, the grass is cut when it grows three inches from the root or once every week. The weeds are picked from the garden and the fountain is cleaned every week. The shrubs are trimmed each month, and the branches from the trees are trimmed away from the house every four months. Pest control and insecticide are administered every three months. Notice the pattern. Naturally occurring things are to be consistently reduced, trimmed away, or wiped clean from the house in these standards to maintain and protect the home. What else can you gather from the example? Did you recognize the boundaries and stipulations? What must an individual be doing to ensure the grass extends no longer than three inches from the root, or various maintenance occur every week, each month, every three months, and every four months? The individual must monitor or keep watch to ensure that the home is sustained. Similarly, setting boundaries for every aspect of your life is a necessity for healthy development. In addition, you must continually monitor those boundaries and uphold the standards put in place for its preservation.

Before we dive into how to create, set, and consistently enforce boundaries, there are a few things to consider. We have covered that healthy boundaries may be difficult to enforce but are healthy and necessary for every relationship in every aspect of life. A healthy boundary will *always* align with the Word of God. When we set and enforce these boundaries, they support our alignment with God, which makes room for an abundance of blessings. An important factor to note is that we are not to set boundaries based on our emotions. Do you remember the discussion about emotions at the beginning of the text? Our emotions are like a thermometer, or an indicator of our mental, physical, and spiritual makeup. So emotions are fickle and shallow, which is why they should have nothing to do with setting a boundary. Since boundaries are set up in every relationship, keep in mind that not everyone will respect your boundaries. You may upset a few people with your boundaries. However, it is not your responsibility to please others. In these instances, remember verses like Galatians 1:10, which reminds us that we were not created to glorify or please other humans but to bring glory to God. We must stay true to the boundaries that we have set. The Bible even tells us how to set and enforce boundaries. Read the scripture below.

¹⁰ As for a person who stirs up division, after warning him once and then twice, have nothing more to do with him, ¹¹ knowing that such a person is warped and sinful; he is self-condemned.
—Titus 3:10–11 (ESV)

This scripture states that if a divisive individual continues to be argumentative over healthy boundaries set in place after two warnings, that individual is to be cut off because of their ungodly nature. Keep in mind that if individuals do not respect the boundaries you have set for them or yourself, it may be that they should not be a part of your life at that time. God may be isolating you for a breakthrough or blessing He has for you.

Sometimes, people set boundaries and standards for others but not for themselves, and vice versa. They must be set for us and for others. I'll use myself in the example of a stranger palming your face. With COVID-19 spiking and killing people daily, I have set strict physical boundaries for my personal space, especially with strangers. So I would be livid if a stranger not only entered my personal space but palmed my face! If I would be angry about an individual violating the boundary set in place, should I go up to strangers to palm their faces? No, I should set a standard to respect other people's personal space just as I would want them to do for me. The Bible backs this up. Read the scripture below.

¹² So in everything, do to others what you would have them do to you, for this sums up the Law and the Prophets.
—Matthew 7:12 (NIV)

Another aspect to consider is the expression of boundaries and standards. Your boundaries and standards must be expressed honestly, clearly, concisely, and out of love. We must remember God's commandment to love Him and love others.

Now let's work on creating boundaries. The first step in creating a boundary is categorization. It sounds harsh, but everyone in your life should have a label. This is how we know what boundaries are needed and the extent of those boundaries to create the necessary standards. Here is a practical example. Do you keep your cleaning products in the pantry with your food? Is your toilet bowl cleaner in the refrigerator next to your milk? How about your insecticides? Do you keep insect repellent in the medicine cabinet? Hopefully, your household cleansers and insecticides are kept separate from the items you consume. Nevertheless, what do all the listed items have in common? Label and categorization. Each item has a label with instructions, warnings, ingredients, and nutrition facts. Also, when we purchase these items, they are categorized. For example, you do not find insect repellent in the refrigerated section next to the milk. In the same way, categorization and labeling are important in creating relational boundaries because every relationship has its place. If we do not categorize an individual correctly, it may result in an unstable relationship. Let's go to the Word of God to confirm categorization. Read the scriptures below.

———————⟫•○•⟪———————

[14] Do not be yoked together with unbelievers. For what do righteousness and wickedness have in common? Or what fellowship can light have with darkness? [15] What harmony is there between Christ and Belial? Or what does a believer have in common with an unbeliever?
—2 Corinthians 6:14–15 (NIV)

Like a muddied spring or a polluted well are the righteous who give way to the wicked.
—Proverbs 25:26 (NIV)

[13] That day Jesus left the house and sat down by the sea side.
[2] Many people came to where he was. So he got into a boat and sat down. All the people stood on the land by the water.
[3] He taught the people many things by telling them stories. He said, `Listen, a man went out to sow some seed.
[4] As he sowed it, some of the seed fell on the road. Birds came and ate the seed.
[5] Some seed fell on the stony ground. Not much earth covered the stones. The seed started to grow right away because it was not deep in the ground.
[6] When the sun began to shine, it was too hot for the new plants. They died because they had no roots.
[7] Some seed fell among the weeds. The weeds grew up and made the new plants die.

*⁸ But some seed fell on good ground. The seed grew and the plants gave more seed.
Some plants gave thirty seeds. Some gave sixty. And some gave a hundred.
⁹ Everyone who has ears, listen!'*
—Matthew 13:1–9 (NIV)

Can you find the categorization and labels in the first scripture? There are believers or unbelievers and wickedness or righteousness that are either with Christ or Belial. (Belial is the personification of the devil.) The scripture challenges the commonality of the labels. Meaning, one of these things is not like the other. Go back to the practical example of the toilet bowl cleaner housed in the refrigerator with the milk. It is the same thing. This scripture gives labels of believer and unbeliever, categorizes those labels as righteous (believer) or wicked (unbeliever), and puts each in their place with Christ (believer) or with the devil (unbeliever). Then a standard is created from the labels and categorization. The scripture explicitly states that these labels (believer and unbeliever) should be categorized or grouped separately. It declares that believers and unbelievers are not to be yoked or linked together. What separates a link? Boundaries.

Let's go to the next scripture. It is short in length but jam-packed with profoundness. Again, the labels are righteous and wicked. However, what is the scripture describing? Is it describing the righteous or the wicked? Which is the muddied spring or polluted well? Notice the juxtaposition that is going on here. Normally, a spring is remarkably clear and good for consumption but is described as muddied in the text. Similarly, a well usually contains drinking water but is described as polluted. The suffix "-ed" in the words "muddied" and "polluted" makes these past tense verbs, which means that they are acts. Something made the clear spring muddy. Something contaminated the well with pollution. What is that "something"? Could it be the wicked? Well, the wicked plays a small part. The two words that let me know this are, "give way." The wicked or toxic influences cannot muddy, pollute, contaminate, or affect us in any way unless we "give way" or allow them to do so. Remember the example of the cottage-style house? When the homeowner *allowed* the things surrounding the house to become overgrown and out of control, it affected both the exterior and the interior of the house. So label and categorize to set boundaries to create standards.

Now the third scripture is slightly different. It is a parable about sowing seeds that categorizes to create standards for interaction. What are the labels in this scripture? We have the road, stony ground, weeds, and good ground. Now what do you think of when you hear sowing seeds? I think of growth and development. The labels in this scripture all reference the ground, which can also be equated to the foundation or the core on which we base our identities. Do you see life growing from streets, roads, or freeways? It is a rare sight, but if you do, it is usually weeds growing from a crack that has occurred to allow it to happen. A stony ground may have some plant life or greenery, but it is short-lived because the rocks prevent growth. Also, the life that does grow in the stony ground quickly sprouts but has shallow roots. It usually dies in the sun's heat. A weed is a surface plant in the wrong place that sucks the life out of surrounding plants. So if sown, weeds will grow but will not conform to or harmonize with the other plants in the garden. In fact, if left unchecked, weeds will stunt the growth of other plants, and overtake and eventually kill other plants in the garden by exhausting all the nutrients for themselves. Lastly, there is good ground. This ground is fruitful and ready for development and growth.

Dr. Anita Phillips preached a sermon called, "Good Ground" that everyone should watch. In that sermon, she teaches that the Bible depicts that we, mankind, are the second generation; plant life is the first (Gen. 1:11, 1:28, NKJV). To further confirm this, she puts up a side-by-side illustration of a human brain stem cell and a seedling. The uncanny resemblance will floor you. So let's break this down to draw a conclusion for this scripture. God finished or completed His creations before He started them. Imagine holding an apple seed in your hand. Because God spoke that fruit would bear seed according to its kind, you are potentially holding an apple tree. A seed grows into a seedling that grows into a plant or tree that produces flowers, vegetation, or fruits. We began as a seed from our earthly fathers that were planted in our mother's womb. Again, even our brain stems resemble plant seedlings. The heart is the subconscious portion of the brain, and change happens by the renewing of our minds. This means that we can all be labeled by one of these four labels: the road, stony, weeds, or good ground. Does the Word of God fall on deaf ears? Have you found yourself thinking that you know better than God? Is your heart too hardened to accept the transformation that God wants to do in your life? This is "the road" in this scripture. Do you hear the Word of God and make changes only to have it faulted by your emotions or your own agendas? Are you jolted by trouble or difficult circumstances? Do you pick and choose what to change instead of totally submitting to God's Will? Are you so consumed with life that God's Word reaches you only at a surface level? This is like the "stony ground" in the scripture. Are you knowingly benefiting from God's goodness and mercy but choosing to live a toxic lifestyle that negatively affects the people close to you? Have you been so badly hurt that you believe your only option is a life filled with toxicity and destruction? This is like the "weeds" in the scripture. Or have you totally submitted to God and all He has for you so that you can grow and develop according to His Will? Does His Love fill you up and overflow unto others? Does your lifestyle support the healthy development of others? Do you live a productive life? This is like the "good ground" in the scripture.

Which category do you fit in? The boundaries and standards we set for ourselves and other people depend on the category. For example, it may not be effective for a believer to regurgitate scriptures to an unbeliever or a person in the road, stony ground, or weeds category because it would either fall on deaf ears or have an adverse effect. That foundation must be cultivated and softened first before sowing the seeds. If you were an expert in astrophysics, would you talk to someone who does not know about astrophysics as if they knew what you were talking about? No, you would start with the principles, the basics, in layman's terms. Also, you would give that individual grace because you know that he/she is unfamiliar with the material or information. It is the same way in life. We should give grace to others out of Love just as God gives grace to us. Remember that grace should also extend to our enemies and people who have hurt us. God commands us to Love. Can you recall what Jesus did for us? Again, He was wounded for our transgressions and died on the cross knowing that we would sin against Him. So we are to Love everyone, but boundaries must be set so that others' positions and offenses do not affect us.

Reflection

Setting boundaries begin with you. What category are you in? Circle your choice below.

The Road   **Stony Ground**   **Weeds**   **Good Ground**

Why did you decide that you are in this category? _____

_____

_____

_____

_____

_____

Apparently, good ground is the ultimate goal of this scripture. It is also apparent that not everyone is on good ground. It is okay if you chose a category other than good ground. There is still time, and you are off to a good start. Also, note that it is possible to be in the "good ground" category but revert to one of the other categories. Fear, our pain, emotions, and experiences have a way of knocking us down at times. We are human. Your honesty is important and plays a vital role in real transformation and wholeness. It is just like the directory maps at a shopping mall or theme park. What is the first thing you do when you walk up to a directory map? You look for the symbol or the words, "YOU ARE HERE." Otherwise, how would you know how to get where you want to be without first knowing where you are now? So let's have a "YOU ARE HERE" moment. Up to this point, we have discussed who God is, who you are in God, and we have addressed your pain and your past. Now, let's put some boundaries and standards in place to build and enforce your development.

Grab your Bible or download a Bible app if you have not done so already. This lengthy series of activities will require you to reference the Bible to ensure that your boundaries are aligned with God. This will serve as a starting-off point for you in creating boundaries for every relationship. So give this major thought. If needed, come back to it and adjust accordingly.

Activity #19a

Think about the people with whom you interact. Make a list of names and label each relationship accordingly. The list can be individuals or a group of individuals. Review the example below.

Example list:

1. Larry, Tanya, and Jane—children
2. Dave—spouse
3. Mom and Dad—immediate family
4. Uncle Buck, Aunt Emm, Cousin Jeff—family
5. Kim and Lorene—close friends
6. Stacy, Brandy, Judy, and Lindsey—friends
7. Sister Nancy, Brother Jim, Pastor Rosco, Pastor Bill (from church)—acquaintances
8. Elizabeth, Mike, and Sue (from work)—work/professional acquaintances

Make your list below.

1. _____
   _____
2. _____
   _____
3. _____
   _____
4. _____
   _____
5. _____
   _____
6. _____
   _____
7. _____
   _____
8. _____
   _____

Activity #19b

Now answer the following questions for each individual or group of individuals listed. Review the example below for guidance.

Categorization Example

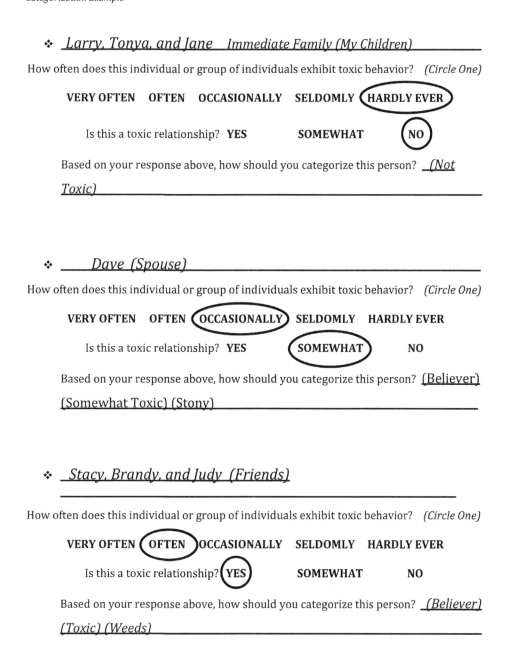

❖ _Larry, Tonya, and Jane   Immediate Family (My Children)_

How often does this individual or group of individuals exhibit toxic behavior?   *(Circle One)*

VERY OFTEN   OFTEN   OCCASIONALLY   SELDOMLY   HARDLY EVER

Is this a toxic relationship? **YES   SOMEWHAT   NO**

Based on your response above, how should you categorize this person? _(Not Toxic)_

❖ _Dave (Spouse)_

How often does this individual or group of individuals exhibit toxic behavior?   *(Circle One)*

VERY OFTEN   OFTEN   OCCASIONALLY   SELDOMLY   HARDLY EVER

Is this a toxic relationship? **YES   SOMEWHAT   NO**

Based on your response above, how should you categorize this person? _(Believer)_ _(Somewhat Toxic) (Stony)_

❖ _Stacy, Brandy, and Judy (Friends)_

How often does this individual or group of individuals exhibit toxic behavior?   *(Circle One)*

VERY OFTEN   OFTEN   OCCASIONALLY   SELDOMLY   HARDLY EVER

Is this a toxic relationship? **YES   SOMEWHAT   NO**

Based on your response above, how should you categorize this person? _(Believer)_ _(Toxic) (Weeds)_

Complete your list below.

❖ _____

How often does this individual or group of individuals exhibit toxic behavior? *(Circle One)*

VERY OFTEN   **OFTEN**   **OCCASIONALLY**   **SELDOMLY**   **HARDLY EVER**

Is this a toxic relationship? **YES**   **SOMEWHAT**   **NO**

Based on your response above, how should you categorize this person? _____

❖ _____

How often does this individual or group of individuals exhibit toxic behavior? *(Circle One)*

VERY OFTEN   **OFTEN**   **OCCASIONALLY**   **SELDOMLY**   **HARDLY EVER**

Is this a toxic relationship? **YES**   **SOMEWHAT**   **NO**

Based on your response above, how should you categorize this person? _____

❖ _____

How often does this individual or group of individuals exhibit toxic behavior? *(Circle One)*

VERY OFTEN   **OFTEN**   **OCCASIONALLY**   **SELDOMLY**   **HARDLY EVER**

Is this a toxic relationship? **YES**   **SOMEWHAT**   **NO**

Based on your response above, how should you categorize this person? _____

❖ _____

How often does this individual or group of individuals exhibit toxic behavior? *(Circle One)*

VERY OFTEN   **OFTEN**   **OCCASIONALLY**   **SELDOMLY**   **HARDLY EVER**

Is this a toxic relationship? **YES**   **SOMEWHAT**   **NO**

Based on your response above, how should you categorize this person? _____

❖ _____

How often does this individual or group of individuals exhibit toxic behavior? *(Circle One)*

VERY OFTEN   **OFTEN**   **OCCASIONALLY**   **SELDOMLY**   **HARDLY EVER**

Is this a toxic relationship? **YES**   **SOMEWHAT**   **NO**

Based on your response above, how should you categorize this person? _____

❖ _____

How often does this individual or group of individuals exhibit toxic behavior? *(Circle One)*

VERY OFTEN   **OFTEN**   **OCCASIONALLY**   **SELDOMLY**   **HARDLY EVER**

Is this a toxic relationship? **YES**   **SOMEWHAT**   **NO**

Based on your response above, how should you categorize this person? _____

❖ _____

How often does this individual or group of individuals exhibit toxic behavior? *(Circle One)*

VERY OFTEN   **OFTEN**   **OCCASIONALLY**   **SELDOMLY**   **HARDLY EVER**

Is this a toxic relationship? **YES**   **SOMEWHAT**   **NO**

Based on your response above, how should you categorize this person? _____

❖ _____

How often does this individual or group of individuals exhibit toxic behavior? *(Circle One)*

VERY OFTEN   **OFTEN**   **OCCASIONALLY**   **SELDOMLY**   **HARDLY EVER**

Is this a toxic relationship? **YES**   **SOMEWHAT**   **NO**

Based on your response above, how should you categorize this person? _____

Activity #19c

Now review your list. The dynamics of each relationship depend on the people. Essentially, there are toxic relationships, which derive from toxic people that facilitate ungodly behavior, just like the "muddied spring" and "polluted well" in Proverbs 25:26. Think about the dynamics of each of the relationships you listed. Can you recognize a pattern? If you categorized the relationship as toxic in any way, where is the toxicity or negativity coming from? Is it the person/people, you, or both? Remember, your honesty is important and plays a vital role in real transformation and wholeness. Jot your answer down somewhere next to the name for your reference.

Activity #19d

Inspect the boundaries and standards you consistently uphold with the relationships you labeled as somewhat toxic or toxic and complete the charts for each. Refer to the "Types of Boundaries" chart that was previously displayed. Review the example charts below for guidance.

Example Chart 1

NAME OR GROUP OF NAMES: Stacy, Brandy, and Judy – Friends (Believers) (Toxic) (Weeds)					
Boundary Category	**Brief Description of Boundaries or Standards Set**	**Clarity** *Are these boundaries Solid & Clear?*	**Healthy** *Do they Aligned with God?*	**Consistency** *Are boundaries set, monitored, or controlled by emotions?*	**Other** *No Boundary Set/Not Applicable*
Physical *refers to the body, privacy, & personal space*	We do not physically fight when we argue. However, we do get in each other's space at times.	No	Not Really	Controlled by Emotions Not Monitored	No Real Boundary Set
Intellectual *views and ideas*	I try to respect them when they make a decision or have ideas, but they often belittle me when I voice my opinions. The arguments become offensive and spew into highlighting each other's past transgressions.	No	No	Controlled by Emotions	N/A
Emotional *separating your feelings from another's feelings*	I don't really have emotional boundaries with them. I thought I could just express myself freely since I have known them for so long. We make up after ever argument.	No	No	Controlled by Emotions	No Boundary Set
Material *Belongings*	We respect, borrow, have access to anything we have except our husbands or significant others.	Yes	Yes	Boundaries are monitored and enforced. Need more boundaries	N/A
Time *Presence, Attention, and Energy*	Time with my family is usually priority and vice versa. I occasionally break this boundary or impede on their time.	Not Really	Yes	Boundaries are not always enforced (Sometimes controlled by emotions) Need more boundaries	N/A

Example Chart 2

NAME OR GROUP OF NAMES: Dave – Spouse (Believer) (Somewhat Toxic) (Stony)					
Boundary Category	**Brief Description of Boundaries**	**Clarity** *Are these boundaries Solid & Clear?*	**Healthy** *Do they Aligned with God?*	**Consistency** *Are boundaries set, monitored, or controlled by emotions?*	**Other** *No Boundary Set/Not Applicable*
Physical *refers to the body, privacy, & personal space*	He does not physically fight me when we argue. However, we do get in each other's space at times. I may shove him when he makes me really angry.	No	No	Controlled by Emotions Not Monitored	No Real Boundary Set
Intellectual *views and ideas*	Sometimes, I respect his decision or ideas, but I let him know when I do not agree. It usually results in an argument. The arguments become disruptive and offensive.	No	No	Controlled by Emotions Boundaries need to be clearly defined and monitored	N/A
Emotional *separating your feelings from another's feelings*	He usually separates his emotions, but I get emotional when we argue.	No	No	Controlled by Emotions	No Boundary Set
Material *Belongings*	I don't have any boundaries with him	No	Yes	No Boundary Set Nothing is monitored. May need to explore.	No Boundary Set
Time *Presence, Attention, and Energy*	He often gets upset that I take away time with my family to spend with my friends. He argues that he is not a priority to me.	Not Really	No	Boundaries are not always enforced. (Sometimes controlled by emotions) Need better boundaries	N/A
Intimacy *Closeness, Togetherness, and Attachment*	We are close, but he wants to be closer. I do not know if I have any boundaries in this category.	?	?	Controlled by Emotions Boundaries need to be set.	No real Boundaries Set

Fill in the charts below.

NAME OR GROUP OF NAMES:					
Boundary Category	**Brief Description of Boundaries or Standards Set**	**Clarity** *Are these boundaries Solid & Clear?*	**Healthy** *Do they Aligned with God?*	**Consistency** *Are boundaries set, monitored, or controlled by emotions?*	**Other** *No Boundary Set/Not Applicable*
Physical *refers to the body, privacy, & personal space*					
Intellectual *views and ideas*					
Emotional *separating your feelings from another's feelings*					
Material *Belongings*					
Time *Presence, Attention, and Energy*					

Fill in the charts below.

NAME OR GROUP OF NAMES:					
Boundary Category	**Brief Description of Boundaries or Standards Set**	**Clarity** *Are these boundaries Solid & Clear?*	**Healthy** *Do they Aligned with God?*	**Consistency** *Are boundaries set, monitored, or controlled by emotions?*	**Other** *No Boundary Set/Not Applicable*
Physical *refers to the body, privacy, & personal space*					
Intellectual *views and ideas*					
Emotional *separating your feelings from another's feelings*					
Material *Belongings*					
Time *Presence, Attention, and Energy*					

Fill in the charts below.

NAME OR GROUP OF NAMES:					
Boundary Category	Brief Description of Boundaries or Standards Set	Clarity *Are these boundaries Solid & Clear?*	Healthy *Do they Aligned with God?*	Consistency *Are boundaries set, monitored, or controlled by emotions?*	Other *No Boundary Set/Not Applicable*
Physical *refers to the body, privacy, & personal space*					
Intellectual *views and ideas*					
Emotional *separating your feelings from another's feelings*					
Material *Belongings*					
Time *Presence, Attention, and Energy*					

Fill in the charts below.

NAME OR GROUP OF NAMES:					
Boundary Category	Brief Description of Boundaries or Standards Set	Clarity *Are these boundaries Solid & Clear?*	Healthy *Do they Aligned with God?*	Consistency *Are boundaries set, monitored, or controlled by emotions?*	Other *No Boundary Set/Not Applicable*
Physical *refers to the body, privacy, & personal space*					
Intellectual *views and ideas*					
Emotional *separating your feelings from another's feelings*					
Material *Belongings*					
Time *Presence, Attention, and Energy*					

Fill in the charts below.

NAME OR GROUP OF NAMES:					
Boundary Category	**Brief Description of Boundaries or Standards Set**	**Clarity** *Are these boundaries Solid & Clear?*	**Healthy** *Do they Aligned with God?*	**Consistency** *Are boundaries set, monitored, or controlled by emotions?*	**Other** *No Boundary Set/Not Applicable*
Physical *refers to the body, privacy, & personal space*					
Intellectual *views and ideas*					
Emotional *separating your feelings from another's feelings*					
Material *Belongings*					
Time *Presence, Attention, and Energy*					

Fill in the charts below.

NAME OR GROUP OF NAMES:					
Boundary Category	**Brief Description of Boundaries or Standards Set**	**Clarity** *Are these boundaries Solid & Clear?*	**Healthy** *Do they Aligned with God?*	**Consistency** *Are boundaries set, monitored, or controlled by emotions?*	**Other** *No Boundary Set/Not Applicable*
Physical *refers to the body, privacy, & personal space*					
Intellectual *views and ideas*					
Emotional *separating your feelings from another's feelings*					
Material *Belongings*					
Time *Presence, Attention, and Energy*					

Fill in the charts below.

NAME OR GROUP OF NAMES:

Boundary Category	Brief Description of Boundaries or Standards Set	Clarity *Are these boundaries Solid & Clear?*	Healthy *Do they Aligned with God?*	Consistency *Are boundaries set, monitored, or controlled by emotions?*	Other *No Boundary Set/Not Applicable*
Physical *refers to the body, privacy, & personal space*					
Intellectual *views and ideas*					
Emotional *separating your feelings from another's feelings*					
Material *Belongings*					
Time *Presence, Attention, and Energy*					

Fill in the charts below.

NAME OR GROUP OF NAMES:

Boundary Category	Brief Description of Boundaries or Standards Set	Clarity *Are these boundaries Solid & Clear?*	Healthy *Do they Aligned with God?*	Consistency *Are boundaries set, monitored, or controlled by emotions?*	Other *No Boundary Set/Not Applicable*
Physical *refers to the body, privacy, & personal space*					
Intellectual *views and ideas*					
Emotional *separating your feelings from another's feelings*					
Material *Belongings*					
Time *Presence, Attention, and Energy*					

Review your charts. Look for patterns or areas of concern. How can you improve boundaries that need improvement? Notate the improved standard for each boundary category as needed. Find scripture to back your answers.

Review the example below.

Boundaries/Standards Chart Example

BOUNDARIES FOR Stacy, Brandy, Judy, and Lindsey - Friends (Believers) (Weeds)

TYPE OF BOUNDARY	REASON FOR BOUNDARY	STANDARD FOR BOUNDARY	CONSEQUENCE FOR VIOLATING BOUNDARY
Emotional	Guard my heart (Proverbs 4:23) The disrespect takes a toll on me and I take it out on others around me.	I will be respectful and honest and demand the same from them. I will stop and intercept gossiping, and demeaning behavior.	I will discuss this with them now. Then, warn them if the boundary is crossed. After that, I will dismiss them as friends. (Titus 3:10-11)
Time	It negatively affects my family, especially my husband, when I allow friends to impede on time designated for us. (Same with my friends' family) Priority Alteration: My husband and I are one flesh (Ephesians 5:31)	I have a duty to my family and must submit to my husband (Ephesians 2:21) My family time and time with my husband will always be priority over friend hangouts.	I will make clear that my family and position in the home comes first. If there is a problem with this, I must discontinue the friendship. (A true friend will understand.)
Intellectual	The tolerated disrespect often results in a more severe level of toxic behavior. "Bad company ruins good morals." (1 Corinthians 15:33)	I must respect them and demand respect in return. Love one another and outdo each other in showing respect. (Romans 12:10)	I will discuss that we must maintain a high level of respect for each other at all times. I will warn them if the boundary is crossed. After that, I will dismiss them as friends. (Titus 3:10-11)

Let's break this example down. Firstly, this example is based on the answers given in boundary chart 1 pertaining to a group of the individual's friends, which has been categorized as believers (believe in God) and weeds (toxic or harmful). We will discuss the first row, which is concentrating on an emotional boundary. Keep in mind that the individual wrote in boundary chart 1 that no emotional boundaries were set for this group of friends. The individual notates the reason for this emotional boundary and gives the scriptural backing for it. Based on this information, the individual sets standards for their friends and herself that will guard her heart and resolve the detriment caused due to the disrespect. Finally, the individual sets up the consequence for violating these standards and impeding on the emotional boundaries in place according to scripture. Again, it may be simple to set up boundaries and standards, but it is often difficult to enforce and maintain them. It can be an overwhelming and intimidating feeling to hold yourself or someone else accountable, especially if you are new to the standards. However, it is well worth it in the long run!

Now complete your charts.

BOUNDARIES FOR _____

TYPE OF BOUNDARY	REASON FOR BOUNDARY	STANDARD FOR BOUNDARY	CONSEQUENCE FOR VIOLATING BOUNDARY

BOUNDARIES FOR _____

TYPE OF BOUNDARY	REASON FOR BOUNDARY	STANDARD FOR BOUNDARY	CONSEQUENCE FOR VIOLATING BOUNDARY

BOUNDARIES FOR _____

TYPE OF BOUNDARY	REASON FOR BOUNDARY	STANDARD FOR BOUNDARY	CONSEQUENCE FOR VIOLATING BOUNDARY

BOUNDARIES FOR _____

TYPE OF BOUNDARY	REASON FOR BOUNDARY	STANDARD FOR BOUNDARY	CONSEQUENCE FOR VIOLATING BOUNDARY

BOUNDARIES FOR _____

TYPE OF BOUNDARY	REASON FOR BOUNDARY	STANDARD FOR BOUNDARY	CONSEQUENCE FOR VIOLATING BOUNDARY

BOUNDARIES FOR _____

TYPE OF BOUNDARY	REASON FOR BOUNDARY	STANDARD FOR BOUNDARY	CONSEQUENCE FOR VIOLATING BOUNDARY

BOUNDARIES FOR _____

TYPE OF BOUNDARY	REASON FOR BOUNDARY	STANDARD FOR BOUNDARY	CONSEQUENCE FOR VIOLATING BOUNDARY

BOUNDARIES FOR _____

TYPE OF BOUNDARY	REASON FOR BOUNDARY	STANDARD FOR BOUNDARY	CONSEQUENCE FOR VIOLATING BOUNDARY

This leads us to our next subcomponent—keeping boundaries or standards through filtration. Having standards for ourselves because of who we are in God means being choosy on *who* and *what* influences us. To do this, we must be mindful of who we hang around, who hangs around us, the content that we put in our minds, the things we listen to, and the material we watch and read. Having boundaries and standards does not mean that we cannot love everyone. Remember, Jesus loves everyone equally, but he did not hang with everyone. He did not allow everyone to influence or affect Him. For example, He only had twelve disciples that He was around, and one of those disciples conspired against Him. This means that everyone is not going to be for you, even the people that are around you in your inner circle. Be careful and selective about who you have in your inner circle. We cannot control other people's outputs and what they say or do, but we can control what we do with those outputs. Will they be filtered for disposal or deposited into our souls? I mentioned Dr. Anita Phillips's filtering system earlier. This would be effective in this instance as well. Filter everything through the Word of God prior to letting it into your mind and heart/soul. Use the Bible like those water filtration systems that hook to the water faucet. It is inevitable that the water will flow from the water faucet. After all, it is a water faucet. However, that filter catches and separates toxins, minerals, impurities, and calcification that contaminates the water. So all that is left is purity, which is suitable and healthy for consumption. In the same way, we must use the Word of God to filter the influences that flow from things in our lives to separate impurities and toxins. Keep in mind that some of these influences can derive from individuals that believe in God. In the scripture below, the apostle Paul is talking to Timothy, telling him to stay away from certain people. Notice that in verse 5, Paul adds that some of the individuals may be believers ("having a form of godliness") but do not behave as such. Read the scripture below.

2 People will be lovers of themselves, lovers of money, boastful, proud, abusive, disobedient to their parents, ungrateful, unholy, 3 without love, unforgiving, slanderous, without self-control, brutal, not lovers of the good, 4 treacherous, rash, conceited, lovers of pleasure rather than lovers of God— 5 having a form of godliness but denying its power. Have nothing to do with such people.
2 Timothy 3:2–5 (NIV)

Therefore, studying and knowing the Word of God is especially important. Each time, answer the question, "Does this align with the Word of God?" If it does, deposit it. If it does not, quickly dispose of it. It is that simple. I say *quickly* dispose of it because we tend to have a habit of holding on to certain offensive things that are done or said to us. Often, we hold on to these things because we believe that it is our duty to address its source to gain justice or reparations for the detriment that the offense may have caused. This begins to weigh on us as it eventually gets deposited in the subconscious part of our mind and affects our actions. Read the scriptures below.

Then He said to the disciples, "It is impossible that no offenses should come, but woe to him through whom they do come!
—Luke 17:1 (NKJV)

¹⁰ And then shall many be offended, and shall betray one another, and shall hate one another.
—Matthew 24:10 (NKJV)

³³ Do not be deceived: "Bad company ruins good morals."
—1 Corinthians 15:33 (ESV)

What are these scriptures saying? Well, let's break each down and read between the lines. The first one states that offenses are inevitable. The second one states that many (not all) will offend, betray, and hate one another. The third one states that bad company ruins good morals. So again, offenses will come. The effects of those offenses are solely up to us. Many will be offended and operate out of God's Will. Betrayal derives from hatred, and hate is the opposite of love. Remember, anyone who does not love does not know God, because God is Love (1 John 4:8 NKJV). So betrayal and hate are out of the Will of God. It is a choice that we must make. Will we allow offenses to enter our mind and heart (our subconscious mind and soul), become offended, and harbor them until it ruins the godly morals within us? Or will we choose to be unoffended by filtering out ungodliness and maintaining our alignment with God?

This is also true for things we choose to expose ourselves to. People, particularly family, friends, and acquaintances, can grossly impact us. Have you ever been around a group of people and realized that your demeanor or mood changed? Have you ever been gaslighted or peer-pressured into doing something that you would not normally do? How about basing a decision on what an individual or group of individuals may say about you? Again, the exposure is inevitable, but it can be filtered and controlled.

I will give you an example from my life. When I was in my early twenties, I thought I had it all together. I had nearly every aspect of my life planned and written down in a journal. I believed that since I was a nice, "good Christian" and did not sin nearly as much as everyone else that God would grant me everything in my journal. I was in college, was a scholar on the dean's list, was in a long-term relationship with my future husband, and had a bright future. Then life happened. My future husband made a mistake that sent him away and significantly altered his life. It was not in my journal of plans, but I stayed and waited for him. Meanwhile, I had family, friends, and acquaintances drilling me with offenses and ungodly advice. It began to eat away at me, transforming me into a bitter person. When my future husband returned, we got married without addressing the traumatic life-altering experiences we had suppressed from each other. We did not secure financial stability. Feelings of entitlement emerged as I allowed other people's highlight reels and accomplishments to send me spiraling into a brutal rage toward my husband. In addition, others were still labeling me as weak, pitiful, and unsuccessful, grouping me with fruitless people, and telling me what I could have had with my substantial potential. Meanwhile, not only was my husband enduring my ruthlessness, but he was also dealing with internal battles that ultimately drove him away from the Will of God. The fact that I did not truly know the glory and power of God and know who I was in Him is why I was unable to filter these offenses. My failure to properly filter these offenses and minimize their offensive influences was the beginning of the end of our marriage.

For am I now seeking the approval of man, or of God? Or am I trying to please man? If I were still trying to please man, I would not be a servant of Christ.
—Galatians 1:10 (ESV)

[1] Blessed is the one who does not walk in step with the wicked or stand in the way that sinners take or sit in the company of mockers, [2] but whose delight is in the law of the Lord, and who meditates on his law day and night.
—Psalm 1:1–2 (NIV)

The media also has a subliminal, profound effect on us. Movies, television shows, the news, social media, and social events are just some examples of things we expose ourselves to. Have you ever found yourself comparing yourself, and your circumstances to fictitious characters or circumstances from movies or television shows? Have you ever changed your viewpoints or countenance on a topic based on the news, a movie, or a television show? Has the media ever caused strong emotions that dictated your behavior? Here is an example. I have never liked scary movies. When I was younger, I was terrified of them, would be filled with anxiety, and lose sleep for days after. However, I discovered a little trick. I knew what I was seeing was not real; it was the startling music and sound effects that got to me. So when my family would watch a scary movie, I would put on headphones to drown out the sound and play music, which would make it less thrilling. I would eventually find myself occupying my time with other activities throughout the movie (writing, drawing, etc.). As long as I covered my ears and could not hear the sound, I could stay in the same room with my family, and it wouldn't affect me. Now the ideal decision would have been to remove me from the room before the movie even started, but we lived in a small, open living space. Sometimes, that is not an option, both in the example and in life. We cannot always immediately remove ourselves from situations. However, we can filter what is deposited and change the tune by focusing on good things.

Have you ever taken a selfie? On average, how many takes does it take to get to that one shot that you post on your social media platforms or stories? I have previously mentioned the highlight reel. The highlight reel is the publicly broadcasted success or accomplishments of others. Even though no human that walks this earth is perfect, people tend to gravitate toward and subliminally allude to perfection. Therefore, people do not usually post things on social media that do not compliment them.

There isn't anything wrong with this. It is not toxic to post photos of your family vacation on social media. You are simply sharing your positive moments with others. It is even okay to retake photos. It is like putting your best foot forward. The problem arises when people that are viewing highlight reels are not comfortable with themselves because they are ignorant as to who God is, do not know who they are in God, or both. This is how the highlight reel can become a negative influence that causes comparison to rear its ugly head and breed ungodly behavior. It goes back to the scripture previously mentioned in the text—2 Corinthians 10:12 (NLT)—which states that individuals that use humans as a standard of measurement to make comparisons are ignorant. So what does this tell us? Bad or toxic influences do not always come from the outside. Practical things can become negative influences if toxicity is already within us. "Toxicity" is another word for contamination. Earlier in the text, we discussed how the fall of Adam left us contaminated, but God sent Jesus to undo that contamination. This goes full circle. Who is the Creator who gave us our identity and purpose? Who is the only One who can undo the contamination? Again, knowing who God is and who you are make all the difference as it establishes standards that prevent you from being influenced by physical or worldly things, keeping you secure and aligned with God.

Why are there commentators for sports events? Football, basketball, and baseball all have commentators that facilitate the game and make it more interesting to describe what's going on. Commentators may get excited and have the influence to excite the crowd. I love going to Houston Rockets games. When the Rockets score, the commentator energetically yells out the name of the Rockets player who made the score, and the crowd goes wild. However, when the other team makes the score, he says the opponent's name and team, but he says it in a low, depressed, almost muffled voice, which brings the energy down in the crowd. The commentator has the power to boost energy and ultimately change the trajectory of the game. This epitomizes the power that the media carries in the world.

Remember, not only are we in the wilderness, but we are also in spiritual warfare. The devil is real, and he is going to come at you three different ways. He will use lust, greed, and pride. So you must be solid in the principles so that he will not penetrate and fool you out of walking toward your purpose.

Look at the illustration below. It represents each of us. God's Spirit and our purpose are embedded deep in our core and are directly correlated with who God is and who we are in God. Because we know who God is, we can discover who we are in God. Because we know who we are in God, we should study His Word. From God's Word, we hold on to the promises and follow the standards that align with His Word. With those standards, we set up and apply boundaries for every relationship in life. And because we know these things and have done all this, the enemy cannot obstruct our purpose. The enemy's schemes are held at bay because we are impenetrable.

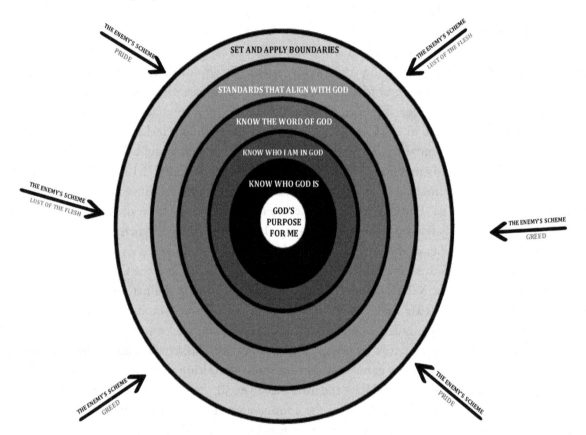

When we are not solidified to know who God is and who we are in Him, we leave ourselves defenseless, which creates gaps, cracks, and blemishes that allow the enemy to delay us from our God-given purpose. The deeper the enemy penetrates *your heart*, the farther away you drift from God and wholeness. The farther away you drift from God, the closer you drift toward ungodliness. Below is an illustration depicting sin invading and disrupting our lives to delay or stop us from fulfilling our purpose. Read the scripture and review the illustration.

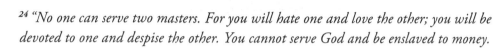

[24] *"No one can serve two masters. For you will hate one and love the other; you will be devoted to one and despise the other. You cannot serve God and be enslaved to money.*
—Matthew 6:24 (NLT)

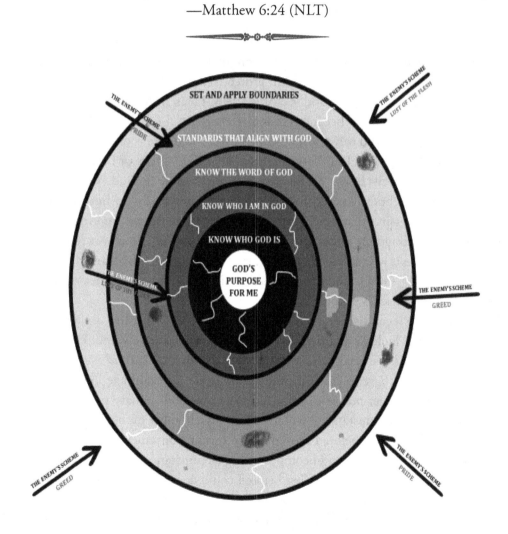

PURPOSE

We have discussed who God is. He is Love, which is an action that is patient, kind, is not envious, not boastful, not proud, not dishonorable, not self-seeking, not easily angered, not petty, not evil but rejoices with the truth, protective, always trusts, hopeful, enduring, and never fails (1 Cor. 13:4–8, NKJV). God is omnipresent. He is always everywhere all at once. So He manifests or reveals Himself because He is already there. God is omniscient, which means that He knows everything and cannot be stumped or shocked. He is omnipotent, which is why we can depend on and lean on Him, knowing that He will never tire or falter. And God is King over all kings, and He dwells in us. We have covered who we are in God. We are a spirit, God's Spirit, clothed in a dirt body, created for His glory to temporarily do business on earth. We prayed the prayer expressing that God is our Lord and Savior. So we are kingdom people; We are residents of God's kingdom, which means we are to follow Kingdom laws found in the Word of God, The Bible. Next, we addressed our past, pain, and struggles by learning how to reframe our situation with BUT GOD. Then, we learned about safeguarding our hearts and mind with boundaries. Now, let's discuss purpose.

Remember, we are second-generation plants (Phillips, 2020). Just like a plant, we were once seeds in the lines of our biological fathers and planted in our mother's womb. However, there was also another seed within that seed … Our purpose is within us. God *did not* place our purpose ahead of us. So we don't have to catch it, wait until we are a certain age for our purpose to be revealed, depending on other people to help us fulfill it, nor do we have to "wait for time to go by" for a more favorable circumstance. I will tell about myself to use me as an example to illustrate this. This book was in me long before I started it, but it was inconvenient for me to start it. I could never seem to find the time, I was in uncompromising circumstances, or I wasn't "mature enough in Christ" yet. So time needed to go by first before I could do what God called me to do. Because I kept finding ways to delay God's instruction, He began revealing things to me that convicted my soul to do the work He has for me because I knew I was wrong. He streamlined my opportunities and dealings to ensure that I had the time to do it. Each time, God's Holy Spirit has ministered to me as I have written this book. Writing this book has increased my thirst for God's Word, has matured me in every aspect of my life as I grow closer to Him, has improved my relationship with others, and has transformed me into a grateful, whole individual who lives to glorify God through service. I could have had that years ago! No, our purpose is not ahead of us, nor is it behind us. Your past is your past and cannot be changed. So there is no need to dwell in the past, as we discussed earlier in the text. Our purpose is a seed within us that will produce good fruit! Do you know why? Well, God created us in His own image (Gen. 1:26, NKJV)! If that isn't enough for you, after God created man, He states that His creation was very good (Gen. 1:31, NKJV). We all came from that first man, Adam!

We are surrounded by purpose! Trees and vegetation create oxygen that we breathe, the sun warms the earth, gives light, and provides vitamin D, and the ants clean the earth. Surely, we have a purpose as well. Purpose is the reason for which something is done or created or for which something exists (*Merriam-Webster*, n.d.). Here is a practical depiction of this. The whole purpose of the game of basketball is shooting the ball through the hoop. So what happens if you take the hoop away? Would there be any point in playing? Basketball would not be basketball as we know it without the hoop. In the same way, life without God is a life that is not worth living because He gives us our purpose. I've stated multiple times that God created us for a purpose. Do you remember this section about God comparing himself to a king? Do you remember a king's glory? Again, we are part of that glory. So it is only logical that God should be #1 priority in our life. The word "priority" derives from the word "prior," meaning existing or coming *before in time, order,* or *importance*. All three apply to who God is to us.

God is committed to the purpose and vision that he has for your life. So you need not worry about failing. God created us as winners. So we must press toward the purpose God has for us by seeking Him. Then, everything else will be added unto us. He has already equipped us with everything we need to fulfill our purpose.

[33] But seek first the kingdom of God and His righteousness, and all these things shall be added to you.
—Matthew 6:33 (NKJV)

Our past is only good for life lessons and educational purposes, which prepares us for our future. Our future is more important than what we have done, what we have been through, and what we were in the past.

¹² Not that I have already obtained this or am already perfect, but I press on to make it my own, because Christ Jesus has made me his own. ¹³ Brothers, I do not consider that I have made it my own. But one thing I do: forgetting what lies behind and straining forward to what lies ahead, ¹⁴ I press on toward the goal for the prize of the upward call of God in Christ Jesus. ¹⁵ Let those of us who are mature think this way, and if in anything you think otherwise, God will reveal that also to you.
—Philippians 3:12–15 (ESV)

According to Dr. Myles Munroe (2017), there are seven steps to a purposeful life.

1. **Purpose.** We are born with our own unique purpose because God gave it to us when He knitted us in our mother's womb.

⁵ "Before I formed you in the womb I knew[chose] you, before you were born
I set you apart; I appointed you as a prophet to the nations."
—Jeremiah 1:5 (NIV)

2. **Vision.** God gives us a vision of our *purpose*. This is where we see our purpose or gain a revelation about our purpose. This is important for *disciplining* our lives.

¹⁸ Where there is no prophetic vision the people cast off restraint, [discouraged]
but blessed is he who keeps the law.
—Proverbs 29:18 (ESV)

3. **Passion.** This is the acceptance of our *purpose* and the drive to complete it. The word "passion" derives from the Latin term *pati*, meaning "suffer." Remember, God promised us that we will have trouble in this life. There will be suffering and sacrifices, which is why we must stand firm on the revelation that God gives us about our purpose, even through difficult times. Remember, we were created for God's glory, not for our own. So when we put in the work, it must always be in the mindset that we are doing it *all* for the glory of God.

---

²³ Whatever you do, work heartily, as for the Lord and not for men, ²⁴ knowing that from the Lord you will receive the inheritance as your reward. You are serving the Lord Christ.
—Colossians 3:23–24 (ESV)

---

4. **Discipline.** The *vision* for our *purpose* narrows our life choices or makes it easier to choose based on the path that gets us to fulfilling our purpose. The word "discipline" derives from the Latin term *discipulus*, meaning "instruction" or "knowledge." Therefore, the knowledge of our purpose through *vision* brings instruction for structure in our lifestyles.

---

12 Whoever loves discipline loves knowledge, but he who hates reproof is stupid.
—Proverbs 12:1 (ESV)

---

5. **Confidence.** Our confidence stems from *passion* for our *purpose* and knowing our path.
6. **Influence.** When we are *confident* and *passionate* about our *purpose*, we are consistently *disciplined*, and our actions begin to rub off on others.
7. **Leadership.** When we gain *influence*, we can begin to lead others and transform their lives through our *purpose*.

Do you see the chain reaction? Each is linked with the other, which simplifies the identification of "kinks in the chain." For example, if an individual lacks discipline, the passion to narrow the lifestyle to align with the vision is missing. Remember, we all have a God-given purpose. So the individual must pursue a closer relationship with God to gain His vision for his or her life. And how will the individual know? He or she must be tuned in to the Holy Spirit for a revelation, by remaining in God's presence. How would the individual remain in God's presence? When the individual knows God, knows who he or she is in God, and safeguards with boundaries and standards to align with God's Word, he or she will dwell in the presence of God.

"The things you got through could kill someone else" (Tony Gaskins, 2021). Gaskins gave a practical example of the purpose and sharing experiences with others by using an analogy of a pothole. Imagine a pothole in the ground. You stumble over the pothole. Although stunned, you walk away with no broken bones or concussion. As others pass, you warn them about that pothole. They are appreciative because they knew they could have broken their leg or failed and broke their neck. In other words, just because you stumbled through a situation and made it doesn't mean that someone else will do the same. The pothole only caused you to stumble, but it could cripple or kill someone else. Situations and crises affect everyone differently. Sometimes your calling may be someone close to you so that he/she/they can reach the masses. And you must be okay with that. I had a problem with this. From the time I was five months pregnant with my daughter, strangers in public would come up to me just to tell me how special the child was that I was carrying. I heard countless times that she is going to change this world. I said earlier in the text that my daughter is on the autism spectrum. She was also diagnosed with anxiety issues. So sacrifices had to be made to nourish and raise my child, my beautiful gift from God. I still create supplemental lesson plans for school, biblical lessons and assignments, and life resource lessons every week. My daughter was unable to hold a simple conversation until she was in the first grade. All her sentences were either directly mimicked by someone else or memorized. Now, at fourteen, she has begun sharing her love for God's Word in creative ways, stands for God's principles in Love, and shares her analogy quotes about life and inspiration. My child is on her way to fulfilling what she was predestined to do. I tried for a while to "have it all" and be omnipresent, but as I stated earlier, I am *not* God! What would have happened if I had neglected my role of motherhood and parenting that God gave me to pursue a more lucrative career? Well, God used me to cultivate the healing and development of my daughter. So the improvements in her development may not have been as significant, which may have delayed her from fulfilling her purpose, which could have delayed the world from receiving something in her gift that it desperately needs. Do you see the ripple effect?

So don't measure or compare your purpose to others. It only causes delays in your destiny. If you believe that your purpose here is greater than most, pride will stunt your progress. If you believe that everyone else's gifts and purpose are more significant, insecurity, another form of pride or self-centeredness, will hinder your progress *(Madu, No crown*, 2021). Don't seek to achieve accolades, seek to be valuable through the purpose that God has given you. Because we all have different purposes and journeys, success is measured *only* by *our* own achievements in the season or period of life God has us in. In other words, did you accomplish what God told *you* to do in the season He has you in? If so, that is a success.

Aside from knowing who God is, discovering your purpose is one of the most important things for an individual to do because discovering your purpose is a part of discovering who you are.

We are creative beings. There are no two people on this planet that are exactly alike. No two people have the exact same fingerprint, genetic makeup, or personality. Fearfully and wonderfully, God created us to be uniquely us for a reason.

The closer our relationship is with God, our Creator, and Purpose Giver, the more He will reveal about ourselves, including our purpose. Purpose can be an overwhelming thing, which is why our omniscient God usually gives it to us in phases or steps. Just imagine being at the bottom of a flight of stairs that stretches 50 stories high. How do you get to the top? (And no, there are no elevators, escalators, or lift supports involved …) Are you just going to leap to the top in one bound? Sure, you can skip a few steps, but that will tire you out in the long run because it requires overexertion of energy. You can sprint up the stairs, but how long would you be able to keep that up? That will most likely result in exhaustion. The best way is to steadily take one step at a time. This is how you gain the momentum needed to press on. You build up that stamina. This is not a 100-meter sprint. This is a marathon. When you skip steps and speed through, you miss out on the momentum you need as you get higher and deeper into your purpose.

11 I have seen something else under the sun:
The race is not to the swift or the battle to the strong, nor does food come to the wise or
wealth to the brilliant or favor to the learned; but time and chance happen to them all.
—Ecclesiastes 9:11 (NIV)

We are supposed to pour ourselves out like a drink offering; we should go to our graves empty, withholding nothing and offering all that God has for us to offer to the world. We have God's spirit inside of us. Remember, God is omnipotent. He's given us power and the potential to contribute to this world. How sad would it be to die, never unleashing or tapping into that potential to make the difference that God created you to make? Tomorrow is not promised.

6 As for me, my life has already been poured out as an offering to God. The time of my death is near.
7 I have fought the good fight, I have finished the race, and I have remained faithful. 8 And now the
prize awaits me—the crown of righteousness, which the Lord, the righteous Judge, will give me on the
day of his return. And the prize is not just for me but for all who eagerly look forward to his appearing.
—2 Timothy 4:6–8 (NLT)

Here is a practical example of untapped potential. Winter storm Uri caused devastation across Texas and Mexico. The aftermath of this deadly storm left over two hundred people dead and $21 billion in damages. Most houses were without lights and water for days. The entire city's water line was shut off. However, about 80 percent of the houses in my neighborhood did not have water after the city turned the water supply back on. So I just assumed I was in that majority. I filled my tubs with water so that we could wash in the sink prior to the water shutting off. We carried water in buckets to transport it. I bought bottled and gallons of water for cooking. Three days later, family and friends stated that they had water the day after the city turned it back on. It still did not register.

It wasn't until an additional two days of "roughing it" that I thought, *I wonder if we have water too.* Sure enough! We had water, both hot and cold! I just neglected to twist the faucet handle to turn it on. We could have been taking showers five days earlier! The potential of hot and cold running water was there but was not utilized. No matter how capable my pipes and faucets were of running water, it did not matter if the act to turn it on was not executed. That's the untapped potential of tap water! Get it? In the same way, we can have all the potential in the world, but it means nothing if we do not utilize it for the advancement of our purpose, what we were created to do.

Reflection

We have a responsibility to fulfill our purpose, to serve and enhance others. What pitfalls in landmines can you warn others about? What gifts can you use to inspire others? What talents do you have that can be offered to the world? How can you encourage others with your story or testimony? How can you pour yourself out as a drink offering to this world where God gets the glory? What legacy will you leave behind for your generation and the generations to come? Notice, I did not mention money, prestige, titles, or material gain because our purpose and value have nothing to do with these fleeting things. So reflect on the questions above without considering financial or material gain.

_____
_____
_____
_____
_____
_____
_____
_____
_____
_____

Don't let hang-ups deter you from your destiny. Don't compare yourself to anyone else on this earth. Your purpose is your purpose. It is unique to you. That's how special you are. God handpicked you to do exactly what He has called you to do. We are not accidents. Nothing just happens. Omniscient, omnipotent, omnipresent, sovereign, perfect. Remember who our God is. He never leaves or forsakes us! And our success is in God's best interest because He is our Creator! We were not meant to fulfill our purpose without God. We are made complete, whole in Christ Jesus. With Him, all things are possible.

CONCLUSION

So here's a list of things we have discussed:

- Who God is
- Why *we* all need God and the invitation to salvation
- Who we are in God
- Acknowledging and addressing our pain and struggles
- Prayer
- Spiritual fasting
- The wilderness mentality
- Boundaries
- Purpose

So I'll bring this to a conclusion by asking some questions. God is omnipotent, omnipresent, omniscient, and sovereign. He is the Creator of all things, and all things are finished when He starts it (Phil. 1:6, NKJV). So can anything in God be incomplete? Can anything or anyone be less than whole? Before God created us, our purpose was already set, and we were tested (Jer. 1:5, NKJV). So the feeling of brokenness and lack and incompleteness must come from a disconnect from the Source (God), which begins in our subconscious minds.

You know that I love my movies. So I will give you one last example from a classic. Do you remember *The Wizard of Oz*? In the movie, Dorothy Gale and Toto were swallowed up in a cyclone and spit out into another world, the Land of Oz. Dorothy and Toto tried throughout the movie to get back to Kansas, their home. They had adventures, obstacles, witches, flying monkeys, and even met friends along the way. One of the biggest obstacles was approaching the Wizard of Oz, who would grant them a request only if they killed the Wicked Witch of the West. Dorothy and Toto wanted to go back home to Kansas, the Scarecrow wanted a brain, the Tin Man wanted a heart, and the Lion wanted courage. Fast-forward to the end, Dorothy and her friends killed the Wicked Witch and returned to the Wizard of Oz, only to find out that he was just an insecure human being masquerading as a powerful wizard. What is worse is that this "wizard" could not grant Dorothy or any of her friends their needs and deepest desires. The wizard could not even help himself, let alone help anyone else! I loved this movie as a small child, but the thing that really agitated me was that the wizard gave the Scarecrow, Tin Man, and the Cowardly Lion trinkets to validate something that they already had. Then Glinda, the Good Witch of the South, told Dorothy that she could have gone home all along by clicking her heels together three times. I would have been so upset! This is life! We are all fully equipped with everything that we need to be successful and live an abundant, purposeful life! God placed it all within us. Just as in the movie, we get so busy doing things to feel complete. Sometimes, people may unwittingly invite us to join them on senseless journeys that have nothing to do with our purpose, just as Dorothy did. Other times, we tag frivolously along on our own. Throughout that movie, each friend exhibited the very things that they *thought* they did not have, which led to them prostituting their qualities for a fruitless cause. The keyword is *thought*. That is our mind. Remember, the way that we think in our hearts is what we are (Prov. 23:7, NKJV). We are already whole! God created *everyone* whole! The disconnect from God has caused us to allow life's problems and struggles to break us, which has resulted in a scarcity mindset and broken heart. The only *one* that can totally restore us is God. We have the gift of free will. As I stated, it's your decision because life is about choice. So choose God's Will for your life and His salvation, find freedom in His principles, live with purpose, and be *whole*.

My Heavenly Father,
Thank You for the opportunity to serve and glorify You. Have
Your Way, God! Manifest and do what only you can do!
It is in the Powerful Name of Jesus I pray this prayer.
Amen.

KEEP GOING!

RESOURCES

Acknowledge Who God Is

King James (KJV). (2008). Retrieved from Bible Gateway: https://www.biblegateway.com/passage

New International Version (NIV). (2008). Retrieved from Bible Gateway: https://www.biblegateway.com/passage

Shirer, P. (2021, November 15). *The Perfect Patience of God | Priscilla Shirer | Social Dallas*. Retrieved from YouTube: Social Dallas: https://www.youtube.com/watch?v=DEVKV9UstR8

Salvation

Munroe, M. (2017, June 20). The Kingdom of God Defined. Retrieved from YouTube: Munroe Global: https://www.youtube.com/watch?v=o6EIWJOQ7qY

Munroe, M. (2018, November 5). Spirit, soul, and body, your greatest trouble. Retrieved from YouTube: Dominion for wisdom: https://www.youtube.com/watch?v=D_7mOXjRvWI

Munroe, M. (2019, January 24). Understanding The Blood Covenant. Retrieved from YouTube: Munroe Global: https://www.youtube.com/watch?v=5X9ZZ02VD_o

Who Does God Say I Am?

Amplified Bible (AMP). English Standard Version (ESV). International Children's Bible (ICB). King James (KJV). New King James (KJV). New International Version (NIV). New Living Translation Version (NLT). (2008). Retrieved from Bible Gateway: https://www.biblegateway.com/passage

Phillips, A. (2020, February 2). Good Ground. *YouTube*. Dallas, Texas, USA: Potter's House. Retrieved from https://www.youtube.com/watch?v=MDCd7LZmOH4

Acknowledge and Address Your Pain

Carter, A. (2021, January 31). Why are you holding onto that? Retrieved from YouTube: Hope City: https://www.youtube.com/watch?v=C9caRCDR0cE

Grace for Purpose. (2021, January 24). Stop Doubting and Keep Praying Until It Happens. Retrieved from YouTube: Grace for Purpose: https://www.youtube.com/watch?v=6oWXQL0h2n0&list=PLCdJUeomK1uVemdhUjC2NPID6BLEANGtE&index=25

Harper, L. (2018, July 16). *When everything falls apart …* Retrieved from YouTube: Elevation Church: https://www.youtube.com/watch?v=wrNtwp5i-IQ

McPherson, M. (2016). Breaking the Silence on Mental Illness. San Diego, California, United States of America. Retrieved from YouTube: Rock Church: https://www.youtube.com/watch?v=rUWzoUWd_3s&list=PLCdJUeomK1uVemdhUjC2NPID6BLEANGtE&index=42

Meyers, Joyce. (2020, May 2). Joyce Meyer Sermons 2020 - "Battlefield of The Mind" (New Sermons Today 2020). Retrieved from YouTube: https://www.youtube.com/watch?v=T33IpdHq_mw

Shirer, P. (2019, May 2). *Going Beyond Ministries with Priscilla Shirer - God Will Use Your Abandoned Boat.* Retrieved from Youtube: Going Beyond Ministries: https://www.youtube.com/watch?v=tJycewWd4bk&t=982s

Prayer

Evans, T. (2019, March 13). Prayer That Works. Retrieved from YouTube: https://www.youtube.com/watch?v=3rXDRl1dQeU

Foster, J. (2019, September 23). Praying Powerful Prayers. Retrieved from YouTube: Hope City: https://www.youtube.com/watch?v=LO-w6cy-sTQ

Munroe, M. (2018, May 30). The Position & Power of Prayer. Retrieved from YouTube: https://www.youtube.com/watch?v=F49cbCIwbuU

Spiritual Fasting

Evans, T. (2018, July 23). The importance of fasting. Retrieved from YouTube: Tony Evans Radio: https://www.youtube.com/watch?v=jze9pnqbK9U

Munroe, M. (2021, January 14). What it means to fast. Retrieved from YouTube: Munroe Global: https://www.youtube.com/watch?v=-IoBw5j1ltY&list=PLCdJUeomK1uVemdhUjC2NPID6BLEANGtE&index=27

The Wilderness

Chan, F. (2021, January 25). Not Everyone Deserves to Be Close to You. Retrieved from YouTube: Francis Chan 2021: https://www.youtube.com/watch?v=nJLzzLHmLj0

Foster, J. (2020, August 23). Balanced Boundaries. Retrieved from YouTube: Hope City: https://www.youtube.com/watch?v=re5028EfYWc

Foster, J. (2020, August 9). Blessing Blockers. Houston, Texas, United States of America. Retrieved from YouTube: Hope City: https://www.youtube.com/watch?v=f8D0seqebQI&list=PLCdJUeomK1uVemdhUjC2NPID6BLEANGtE&index=36

Madu, R. (2021, February 1). No Crown: Sermon series "No Cap." Dallas, Texas, United States of America. Retrieved from YouTube: Social Dallas: https://www.youtube.com/watch?v=WeXra4C4AUs&t=2657s

Munroe, M. (2019). Control Your Mind. Retrieved from YouTube: https://www.youtube.com/watch?v=GGfaLYKMHWs&list=PLCdJUeomK1uVemdhUjC2NPID6BLEANGtE&index=43

Selva, J. (2020, October 16). How to Set Healthy Boundaries: 10 Examples + PDF Worksheets. Retrieved from PositivePsychology.com: https://positivepsychology.com/great-self-care-setting-healthy-boundaries/

Sentis. (2012, December 11). Conscious vs. subconscious thinking. Retrieved from YouTube: https://www.youtube.com/watch?v=UYSKW3IvZlQ

Purpose

Gaskins, T. (2021, April 18). *Your purpose is bigger than you*. Retrieved from Youtube: Tony Gaskins: https://www.youtube.com/watch?v=-l1oRm7FHMI&list=PLCdJUeomK1uVemdhUjC2NPID6BLEANGtE&index=29

Gaskins, T. (2021, July 11). Prayers, position, and preparation! Florida, United States of America. Retrieved from YouTube: Tony Gaskins: https://www.youtube.com/watch?v=Bx4PkXisrmQ&t=287s

Madu, R. (2020, April 7). Water and the Wilderness. YouTube. Retrieved from https://www.youtube.com/watch?v=xt62IADvC2Q

Munroe, M. (2017, December 2). Activate your hidden potential [Recorded by M. Munroe]. Bahamas. Retrieved from YouTube: https://www.youtube.com/watch?v=BN5X_gW8_h0

Todd, M. (2021, Jun 13). *Michael Todd: Your Pain Prepares You for Your Purpose*. Retrieved from YouTube: TBN: https://www.youtube.com/watch?v=8MWLFnw6bw4&list=PLCdJUeomK1uVemdhUjC2NPID6BLEANGtE&index=16

Other

DeRamus, T. (2017, February 16). Exploring the Fundamental Needs of the Human Mind. (TEDxLSCTomball, Editor) Retrieved from TEDx Talk: https://www.youtube.com/watch?v=nw6u3fk88pY

Martin, A. (2021, August 20). United States Department of Agriculture (USDA). Retrieved from Food Prices and Spending: https://www.ers.usda.gov/data-products/ag-and-food-statistics-charting-the-essentials/food-prices-and-spending/

Online Etymology Dictionary. (2021). Online Etymology Dictionary. Retrieved from Online Etymology Dictionary: etymonline.com/

Printed in the United States
by Baker & Taylor Publisher Services